MW01144394

# CONTENTS

CERTIFICATE

DECLARATION

ACKNOWLEDGEMENTS

DETAILED CONTENTS

LIST OF ABBREVIATIONS

LIST OF TABLES

LIST OF CHARTS

## ACKNOWLEDGEMENTS

I wish to place on record, with a sense of pride and achievement, my immense gratitude to **Dr.A.GUNASEKARAN**, Reader and Head, Post Graduate and Research Department of Economics, Sir Theagaraya College, Chennai-21, whose benevolent guidance, kind support and constant encouragement immensely helped me to the preparation and presentation of the thesis.

I wish to express my profound thanks to former and present Principal, Sir Theagaraya College, Chennai-21, for the opportunity given to me to pursue my research work in the college. It is my bounden duty to acknowledge my gratitude to the faculty member of the Department of Economics, Sir Theagaraya College, Chennai-21 for their gracious and generous assistance.

I am highly indebted to **Dr. R. THANDAVAN**, Professor and Head, Anna Centre for Public Affairs, University of Madras, Chennai-5, for being a source of inspiration to pursue my doctoral study.

A special note of thanks to **Mr.Muralidharan**, Regional Area Manager, Salem and **Mrs. Bharathi**, Regional Area Manager, Chennai Branch for providing all the data required for this work. I also thank the beneficiaries whom I approached to complete the Questionnaire for my study.

My venerable thanks are to the Librarians and the Staff of the University of Madras Library, Chennai, Institute of Financial and Management Research

Library(IFMR), Chennai, British Council Library, Chennai and Connemara Library, Chennai.

I owe to lot to my parents and my husband for their continuous support, patience and encouragement given to me throughout my work.

V. Charulatha
**(V.CHARULATHA)**

# DETAILED CONTENTS

# LIST OF ABBREVIATIONS

| | | |
|---|---|---|
| ALM | - | Asset Liability Management |
| CBD | - | Central Business District |
| CMA | - | Chennai Metropolitan Area |
| CMDA | - | Chennai Metropolitan Development Authority |
| CIT | - | City Improvement Trust |
| CRISIL | - | Credit Rating and Information Services of India Limited |
| CPWD | - | Central Public Works Department |
| DDA | - | Delhi Development Authority |
| ESI | - | Employees State Insurance |
| EWS | - | Economically Weaker Sections |
| EMI | - | Equated Monthly Instalment |
| GSE | - | Government Sponsered Enterprises |
| GSS | - | Global Strategy for shelter |
| GIC | - | General Insurance Corporation |
| GDP | - | Gross Domestic Product |
| HFI | - | Housing Finance Institution |
| HUDCO | - | Housing and Urban Development Corporation |
| HFC | - | Housing Finance Company |
| HDFC | - | Housing Development Finance Corporation |
| HLA | - | Housing Loan Account |
| HIG | - | High Income Housing Group |
| IFC | - | International Finance Companies |
| IRDP | - | Insurance Regulatory and Development Authority |
| ICICI | - | Industrial Credit and Investment Corporation of India |
| IAY | - | Indira Awas Yojna |
| IT | - | Information Technology |
| KYC | - | Know Your Customer |
| LIC | - | Life Insurance Corporation |
| LICHFL | - | Life Insurance Corporation Housing Finance Limited |
| LIG | - | Low Income Group |
| MMDA | - | Madras Metropolitan Development Authority |
| MRTS | - | Mass Rapid Transit System |
| MIG | - | Middle Income Group |
| MNP | - | Minimum Needs Programme |
| NHB | - | National Housing Bank |
| NBO | - | National Building Organisation |
| NCU | - | National Commission of Urbanization |
| NRI | - | Non Resident Indian |
| PF | - | Provident Fund |
| RBI | - | Reserve Bank of India |
| RRB | - | Regional Rural Banks |
| SAARC | - | South Asian Association for Regional Co-operation |

| | | |
|---|---|---|
| SPV | - | Special Purpose Vehicle |
| SLR | - | Statutory Liquidity Rate |
| | | |
| TNHB | - | Tamil Nadu Housing Board |
| UNCHS | - | United Nations Centre for Human Settlements |
| UTI | - | Unit Trust of India |
| UK | - | United Kingdom |
| USA | - | United States of America |

## LIST OF TABLES

## LIST OF CHARTS

# INTRODUCTION

# CHAPTER I

## INTRODUCTION

Proper Housing is an important need for every human being. It is a vital need after food and clothing. A certain minimum standard of housing is essential for healthy and civilized existence. Proper accommodation for a human being depends upon utilization of resources and economic well being. Housing helps in gaining social status and acceptance and also helps in urban growth, income distribution etc. Increasing gap between the availability and demand for housing is the root cause for homelessness in the modern times.

Housing is a package of shelter and services. It must thus also be reviewed in terms of substitution and contemprarity.[1] Housing is a challenging problem for an urban community. Poor housing is the most serious manifestation of mass poverty and reflects the economy of the country. A cursory glance at our urban housing needs and scarcity of resources presents a picture of the serious problem and its magnitude. The programmes of mass housing for urban poor have not been realized as there is no needful attention in a planned strategy, unintended settlements and squatter colonies have increased in alarming proportions.

The standard of living of a society can be judged by the adequacy of housing and housing conditions, which help to determine the immediate environment of human settlements. Barring a few countries, most of the countries in the world have ensured adequate supply of food needed for their subjects; sufficient progress and

---

[1] HOUSING SECTOR POLICY, **World Bank**, p.2.

headway have been achieved in this front. But in housing no significant headway has so far been achieved and India is no exemption to this universal phenomenon. Housing programme lags far behind industrial progress in every part of the world.[2] It is undeniable fact that investment in housing is an important means in the economic upliftment of a country as it helps in creating better employment opportunities as housing involves construction works and is highly labour intensive. Housing is so essential that it provides satisfaction, status, privacy, security and equity as well as shelter for the owners. It plays a significant role in shaping the life style of an individual and moulding the future of the society. The house is a secured place to live in with dignity. Shelter through housing is an intrinsic part of human settlement, and it is closely linked with the process of overall socio-economic development.

In majority of the developing countries there is an increasing gap between availability and demand for housing. Growth of population in the developing countries is on the increasing side. Population growth has a market effect on the structure of demand for housing.[3] The Census of the year 2001 has revealed that the Indian population, which had been estimated to cross the billion mark by the turn of the Century, had touched 1027 millions as in March 2001. This growth concentrated more in the urban areas in the country. The sheer scale of the growth in population poses a severe task for builders and promoters. Housing is an essential requirement of life for every human being. More construction of houses and development activities accounts as major indicator of the prosperity of a nation.

---

[2] CHARLES ABRAMS, **Housing in the modern world,** (London Faber and Faber 1966), p.51
[3] GIRIAPPA S., **Housing Finance and Development in India,** (Mohit Publications, New Delhi, 1998), p.4.

In all the developed and developing countries housing is one of the principal factors that affect the level of living status of the people. It plays a multiple role in creating employment and economic growth in maintaining health and social stability and in preserving the values of decent family life. Housing is of particular importance to a country like India where employment is a very serious problem.[4] Housing also contributes to the physical environment that is society's basic unit on which the family develops. The improvements of this physical environment represent a concrete and visible rise in the general level of living. Initially, United Nations documents were the first that explicitly mentioned about the right of housing in the Universal Declaration on Human rights which states that:

"Everyone has the right to a standard of living adequate for the health and well being of himself and of his family, including food, clothing, housing and medical care and necessary social services. (Article 25(1)". Since the adoption of this declaration in 1948, the human right to adequate housing has been repeatedly reaffirmed. The Vancouver Declaration on Human Settlements and Plan of Action (1976) included reference to a range of individual human rights, State based rights and other legal provisions. The Global Strategy for shelter in the year 2000 (GSS) further reinforced the right to adequate housing and the obligation of nations to ensure an enabling environment in the shelter sector."[5]

---

[4] FRANCIS CHERUNILAM & ODEYAR D. HEGGADE, **Housing in India**, (Himalaya Publishing House), p.28.
[5] SERIES OF PUBLICATIONS IN SUPPORT OF THE GLOBAL CAMPAIGN FOR SECURE TENURE NO.3/2000 **"Strategies to combat homelessness"** (United Nations Centre for Human Settlements (Habitat), Nairobi, 2000, Publishing Unit), p.3

The shortage of finance for housing has been recognized as one of the hindrances to the provision of housing for different households. Currently for every house built, funds utilized are from formal financial institutions, another three to five houses are built with personal savings and funds from other informal sources. Housing finance is inter-dependently linked with the provision of infrastructure and utilities because of its intense relationship with the volume construction to be built. From the conceptual foundation, one can see housing finance occupying a crucial intermediary role between production cum construction of new building, consumption of raw materials for the construction and the arrangement of finance for it or the economy on one hand, and the housing system on the other.

Housing credit and mortgages have a connection between the supply of housing for the purchaser to the demand of the households. Accessibility to credit and instalment purchase becomes very important. Eligibility for accessing credit depends on the duration of loan, the rate of interest and the amount of deposit, which is required as down payment made at the initial stage by the applicant or the purchaser.

Housing finance is the capital made available to the household to improve or acquire a house. Acquiring a house means building a house or buying one that has been built by someone else. Housing consumption is financed by a combination of two types of capital funds. One consists of internal sources of funding, which derive primarily from the savings of individuals or groups of investors, and are normally represented by down payments on housing. The second source consists of external funding, primarily from institutions, which is obtained as credit through mortgages.[6] The house can be bought from any number of sources including the builder or promoter, independent house owner or from a landlord and the seller may be an individual or an institution. The amount of housing finance required will depend primarily on the gap between the cost of acquisition and the amount already available with the purchaser. However demand can only become effective if the purchaser is able and willing to borrow the amount.

In India, initiative for developing housing projects had begun with the First Five Year Plan. The Plan gave priority and formulated plans to provide successive construction of standard housing facilities in the country. The National Housing policy of 1988,1991 and the National Housing and Habitat policy of 1998 were an action plan drawn to achieve the target of "Shelter for all" enunciated in the national agenda. The National Housing Policy stated easy access to institution finance at affordable rates as a pre- requisite for accelerating housing investments.[7] The central theme of the policy strengthens the public and private partnership for tackling the housing and infrastructure problems faced by the country. The policy provides fiscal concessions, with legal and regulatory and creates an enabling environment for the construction of houses in the country.

Construction activity plays an important role in the development of various industries and in the generation of employment opportunities. On the demand side, softening of lending rates and increase in income levels coupled with the tax

[6] LARRY S.BOURNE, **The Geography of housing**, (Edward Arnold publishers Ltd., London, 1981), p.116.
[7] POLICY NOTE, **department of housing**, (Government of Tamilnadu, Madras,1991), p.6.

incentives given by the central government have led to significant increase in off take in housing finance. With the housing finance sector receiving due importance, it is witnessing increased competition with larger number of players particularly banks trying to garner higher market share by offering an array of home loan products at competitive and many a times lower rates facilitated by their lower cost of funds, placing the housing finance companies at a slightly disadvantageous position.[8]

There has been a phenomenal growth in the demand for housing in the country in recent years both in quantitative and qualitative terms due to increase in population, expansion of industrial and commercial activities, large-scale immigration into urban areas etc.[9] Taking into consideration the importance of housing for the people and for the economic development of the nation the Government of India has given priority for this sector in all five-year plans. Surprisingly, the five-year plans have not duly recognized the importance of housing in terms of significant levels of investment. From the very inception of our five-year plans, it has been observed that the priority in planning strategy for an orderly investment in housing is lopsided.[10] Thus housing has not been regarded as a productive source of investment.

In the First Five Year Plan, the efforts were restricted to a limited section of society and schemes included subsidized industrial housing, low-income housing and provisions of housing for plantation, coal and mica mine-labourers. Expansion of

---

[8] EXCERPTS FROM THE CHAIRMAN SPEECH, **LIC Housing Finance Limited,** (Annual General Meeting, 2001).
[9] Vidhyavathi K, **Role of Urban Housing Finance Institutions in Karnataka,** (Finance India, VolXVI No.1, March 2002), p.242.
[10] Rajalakshmi N, **Tamilnadu Economy,** (Business Publications), p.155.

support to institutional agencies and intensification of research and development of cheap materials were framed as objectives of the First Five Year Plan.

This programme was further expanded in the Second Five Year Plan, which encompassed three new programmes in rural housing, slum clearance and sweepers housing and middle income group housing. Under the Second Plan, a few schemes were taken up for slum clearance and slum improvement, village housing and land acquisition and development. A few other specific schemes were also designed to benefit the weaker sections of the community like scheduled castes, scheduled tribes and backward classes in rural areas, handloom weavers and displaced persons etc.

Setting up of housing policies for the economic development and industrialization, coordinating the efforts of all the housing agencies namely public, cooperative or private, and creation of the entire programme of housing construction to serve specially the requirements of the low income groups are the measures taken during the Third Five Year Plan.

The fourth plan proposed that the private sector should standardize building components and manufacture them on a large scale. Encouragement has been given to co-operative effort. Special housing schemes in favour of scheduled castes and other weaker sections were also mooted.

The Fifth Five Year Plan emphasized the role of housing in economic development, both as an end and a means. As an end, housing is an essential ingredient in the basic requirements of civilized living; as a means, besides adding to national income, housing is a strong motivator of saving and plays an important part in the generation of employment.[11] The Plan observes that emphasis should be on limiting the rise in the prices of land, providing financial assistance to co-operative and private effort and assuming legal powers for reconditioning of slums.[12]

The sixth plan aimed at reducing substantially the number of absolutely shelterless people and at providing conditions for others to improve their housing environment. Provision of house sites and assistance for the construction of dwellings for rural landless labourers, designing the public sector housing schemes to benefit the economically weaker sections of the community, augmenting the resources of institutional agencies like HUDCO and State Housing Boards to enable them to provide infrastructural facilities as a means of encouraging in the private sector, special efforts to secure a reduction in costs in public housing schemes by reviewing standards and by using cheap and alternative building materials were the primes aims of the Sixth Five Year Plan.

A major objective of the Seventh Plan is to strengthen the financial infrastructure for housing.[13] The Seventh Plan focuses on promotion and encouragement of self-help housing, providing assistance for construction, dwelling for those rural families who had already been provided house sites, providing stimulus and support for private housing for the middle and lower income groups so as to channel increased savings into housing, harnessing science and technology efforts for improving building technology and development of cheap and local building materials.

[11] Sharma O.P., "**Housing the houseless: Time Ripe for action**", (The Economic Times, December 1975).
[12] Planning Commission, **Fourth five year plan**, p.402
[13] Vinay D. Lall, **Housing Finance in the Seventh plan perspective**, (Indian Institution of Public administration, New Delhi, Indraprashta Estate Ringh Road, 1989), p.206.

The Eighth Plan explicitly recognised the role and importance of the urban sector for the national economy. The Plan identified the key issues in the emerging urban scenario, viz: the widening gap between demand and supply of infrastructural services, which hits the poor, whose access to the basic services like drinking water, sanitation, education and basic healthcare is shrinking; the unabated growth of the urban population, aggravating the accumulated backlog of housing shortages and resulting in the proliferation of slums and squatter settlements and decay of city environments. An important development in the Eighth Plan was the bringing about of a consensus in the approach to human settlements development.[14]

Having identified housing as a priority area in the Ninth Five Year Plan (1997-2002), the National Housing Policy has envisaged an investment target of Rs. 1,500 billion for this sector. In order to achieve this investment target, the Government needs to make low cost funds easily available and enforce legal and regulatory reforms.

In India, the housing economy is intertwined with the macro economic scenario through its numerous forward and backward linkages both on the supply as well as the demand side. On the one hand, favourable budgetary policy pronouncements and legislative reforms facilitate enhanced supply while expansionary fiscal and monetary policy incentives encourage increase in effective demand for housing by enhancing disposable income and reducing the effective cost of borrowing.[15]

---

[14] NABHI'S PUBLICATION OF **Ninth Five Year Plan (1997-2002)**, (A Nabhi Publication), p.599.
[15] REPORT ON TREND & PROGRESS OF **HOUSING IN INDIA**, (June 2001), p. 3.

According to the National Building Organisation (NBO), the total demand for housing is estimated at 2 million units per year and the total housing shortfall is estimated to be 19.4 million units, of which 12.76 million units is from rural areas and 6.64 million units from urban areas. The housing industry is the second largest employment generator in the country. It is estimated that the budgeted 2 million units would lead to the creation of an additional 10 million man-years of direct employment and another 15 million man-years of indirect employment.

## HOUSING AND FINANCE

Many of the present ills of the society can be traced back to the sprawling urbanization and consequent unprecedented pressure on the existing housing stock and infrastructure. The shortage of houses is felt more acutely in the urban areas than in rural areas, where due to the present trend of industrial growth, people from countryside migrate to towns in large numbers.

India, after independence, did recognize the above aspects and took earnest and concrete efforts to provide housing facilities to the increasing population. The Government weeded to the concepts of a welfare state and thought of housing the masses, mostly the slum dwells, industrial workers in the low income group in hygienic environments.

Housing construction and finance is a significant driver of economic growth in developed and developing countries alike. The sector includes construction firms as well as industries supplying building materials, components, and products for interior design. But home building flourishes only where there is a robust market for housing finance. A well-functioning housing finance system typically has a catalytic impact on banking activities, household savings, and capital markets activities that link long-term investors with residential mortgage consumers of credit.

International Finance Companies (IFC) helps to increase the availability and affordability of residential housing in developing countries. This focus includes enabling adequate supply of appropriate housing stock and the sustainable mobilization of capital. IFC also helps overcome obstacles to housing finance markets in developing countries, including.

- Lending restrictions
- Lack of financial infrastructure
- Legal and regulatory constraints
- Limited institutional capacity
- Lack of access to construction finance

Nearly one half of the world's urban population lives in poverty and about 800 million people occupy substandard housing. This "housing crisis" has continued unabated despite over 20 years of research and policy. Various policy initiatives confirmed that the provision of small quantities of finance to low-income households will bring real improvements to the quality and quantity of housing provision. Both public and private formal finance institutions have experienced great difficulty in lending below a middle-income client group, and are often reluctant to lend for the purpose of housing at all.

The housing finance market is among the most important in the finance market. It accounts for a sizable portion of the production activity of a country, through its backward linkages to land markets, building materials, tools, durable goods, and labour markets.

Housing markets have significant forward linkages with financial markets, as well. Mortgage debt accounts for a large proportion of household debt and, through secondary markets and securitization, supports the efficient functioning of domestic and international financial markets. Housing markets are routinely monitored as an important leading indicator of overall macroeconomic activity. The housing finance sector has a tremendous developmental impact, both in terms of providing social stability and in promoting economic development.

## SOCIAL STABILITY

Housing Finance contributes to social stability by enabling households to purchase an asset, which will represent their largest single investment. Personal residences account for 75% to 90% of household wealth in emerging market countries, which amounts to 3 to 6 times their annual income. Furthermore, housing represents 15% to 40% of the monthly expenditure of households worldwide. Investment in housing accounts for 15% to 35% of aggregate investment worldwide. By supporting housing finance, the IFC promotes a successful economic sector and frees personal savings, which entrepreneurs can invest in small businesses. Housing construction and housing related sectors constitute approximately 9% of the labour force worldwide.

## GROWTH OF HOUSING FINANCE SECTOR

The housing finance industry is considered the most viable of all financing business, secured by the immovable asset itself. About two decades ago, the housing finance industry was dominated by a single private sector housing finance company(HFC). There are about 383 Housing Finance Companies in India today with the entry of banks making the business competitive. The housing finance industry is regulated by the National Housing Bank(NHB), a subsidiary of the Reserve Bank of India(RBI). The Reserve Bank of India, through the National Housing Bank, issues guidelines for the housing finance sector covering key issues, namely the sourcing of funds, disbursement areas, risk weightage and provisioning norms, among others. Tenure of home loan is among the longest when compared with other financing businesses. The average maturity of home loan is about 15 years, primarily to make it affordable.

## SIGNIFICANCE OF STUDY

Housing finance represents a large share of total capital formation and is important for development at all levels in both economic and welfare aspects. Towards the end of the last decade housing sector has gained importance. In Chennai city, the aspirants for owning a house, have been increased recently especially by the middle class people. They are said to be the main targets by many housing financial institutions. To fulfill the needs of such aspirants, LIC Housing Finance Ltd., one of the main financial institutions in India has involved in the activity of providing housing finance.

In this context the research study focuses on housing finance as the main theme and an attempt has been made to study the performance and approaches of LICHFL in providing financial assistance for housing and to know the level of satisfaction of the borrowers, besides identifying the problems of borrowers and their opinions.

## HOUSING FINANCE INSTITUTIONS

The housing finance industry comprises of about 383 firms from both private and public sector. Of these, most of the business nearly 95 per cent of it is restricted to 26 institutions which have these disbursements refinanced by National Housing Bank (NHB), the regulatory body of the sector.

There was a time given the normal cultural practice, taking a loan was frowned upon. Worst situation would be restricted to friends or from place of work. Ten years ago, if one had wanted to buy a house there were only a handful of loan providers to choose from Housing Development Corporation Limited, LIC housing Finance, Canfin homes, Housing and Urban Development Corporation Limited and the like. The entry of aggressive new players over the last few years has changed the landscape of housing finance. The housing loan business is the largest asset business in the bank.

The importance given to life of the individuals necessitated the establishment of LIC and the importance of housing for such lives leads to the incorporation of LIC Housing Finance with the control of Life Insurance Corporation. LIC housing Finance has come a long way since inception to grow into mega saviour of welfare economics in providing housing finance. In the last two decades, the company has developed extraordinary goodwill and patronage among public in all directions in providing housing finance not only the individuals, but also to the other borrowers.

Since the incorporation the overall sanctions and disbursements of loans has shown a tremendous growth.

The main objective of the company is to carry on the business of providing long term finance to any person or persons, company or corporation, society or association and in particular, to holders of policies issued by the Life Insurance Corporation Housing Finance (LICHF), enabling such borrower to construct or purchase a house or flat for residential purposes. The Security upon such security and such terms and conditions as the company may deem fit and to also provide long term finance to persons engaged in the business of construction of houses or flats for residential purpose. The same to be sold by them by way of hire purchase or on deferred payment or other similar basis upon such terms and conditions as the company may think fit and proper.

LIC Housing Finance supplemented its reach through Life Insurance Corporation's strong agency network. The company encouraged borrowers to cover themselves with life insurance-protect repayments and ensure a continued ownership of the house by members of the borrower's family in the event of an unforeseen mishap. As a result, the insurance policy worked as an effective collateral. Since there was a commonality of interest between LIC Housing Finance and its parent in this area, Life Insurance Corporation's vast agency network also marketed the housing schemes of LIC Housing finance.

Over the last few years, competition in the housing finance industry has increased manifold from other housing finance companies and banks. Although banks enjoy a cheaper source of funds, an housing finance company like LIC Housing

Finance enjoys some advantages that banks lack, viz a stronger core competence, years of experience, increased customization, a deep reach and a greater trustability among its stakeholders. Besides, in the opinion of the management, once the economy revives, banks could re-allocate a larger portion of their resources to their core business, whereas companies like LIC Housing Finance would have a sustainable and therefore, more credible presence.

## STATEMENT OF PROBLEM

In India, housing finance poses a big problem in building one's own dwelling unit as self savings cannot be made adequate to solve the housing problem overnight. Most of the people who might have been living in rental houses quite a long period would like to construct their own houses. Speculative land prices and spiraling rents with fluctuating situations further worsened the housing problem in the urban areas. The demand for housing finance is agglomerative in nature with rapid population growth and necessitates the Government to take relevant measures to meet such demand.

Migration of people from rural areas to urban areas to perceive an opportunity of earning a higher income and living a better life in a city leads to housing shortage in urban areas. The present housing finance companies and banks are proved to insufficient to cater to the urban housing requirements. The housing problem is further complicated by economic backwardness, skyrocketing prices, rising costs of real estate and construction and the housing needs in terms of location, size, tenure, type or facilities are not met with.

An inadequate attention or low preference has paid towards the housing sector inspite of its indispensable role in the economic development of the country. Institutional funds get locked up since amortisation of principal is very slow and problems tend to arise out of lack of funds with no alternative means for raising funds to meet the proliferating financial needs for urban housing.

There are many housing finance institutions and banks issuing so many schemes under different terms and conditions to be compiled with. The borrowers find difficult in selecting the appropriate loan scheme to suit his financial requirements in terms of the quantum of loan and interest rates with adequate repayment terms. The long term finance needed for housing would be practically not available because of the highly sophisticated and lengthy legal procedure which has to be strictly followed. In these circumstances, an attempt is made in this research work to study the performance of LICHFL in providing the housing finance.

**OBJECTIVES**

A sincere adherence is made to the following objectives in order to conduct this research study.

1. To trace the housing finance system and policies in India.

2. To analyse the changing role of housing financial institutions

3. To review the performance of the operational and financial position of LIC Housing Finance Limited.

4. To elicit the opinion of the urban beneficiaries of LIC Housing Finance Limited.

5. To suggest the measures to improve the efficiency of LIC Housing Finance Limited.

**HYPOTHESIS**

The important hypotheses of the study are:

1. There is a significant increase in the disbursal of housing loan by the LIC Housing Finance Ltd.

2. There is a significant improvement in the financial position of LIC Housing Finance Ltd.

3. The beneficiaries are happy with the services provided by LIC Housing Finance Ltd.

4. The beneficiaries are aware of the rules of the LIC Housing Finance Ltd.

5. There is a significant difference in the opinion of the beneficiaries on their loan requirement and loan sanctioned by the LIC Housing Finance Ltd.

**PERIOD OF STUDY**

The Secondary data of the present study covers the period from 1996 to 2006.During this study period, recognizing the importance of shelter the SAARC has announced the year 1997 as the year of shelter insisting the need of housing for the people in developing Asian countries. This study period covers Ninth Five year National Plan and the Tenth Five Year Plan in India. The primary data for the study covers the period between 2005 and 2006.

**METHODOLOGY**

Chennai city has been chosen as the broad study area for the purpose of this research. There were about 50 financial institutions of varying size in Chennai city offering loans for the purchase of houses/flats. Both primary and secondary data were collected for the study.

The sample size consisting of 300 beneficiaries of LIC Housing Finance Limited in Chennai city was randomly selected during 2005-2006. Based on the objectives, aquestionnaire was designed for the LICHFL beneficiaries to identify the personal demographics, social economic factors, loan areas, repayment of loan, tax incentives, etc. The opinion of the beneficiaries over the effective functioning of the LICHFL and suggestions were also collected.

Secondary data was collected from various reports, Manuals, Journals, Materials, published by Central and state Governments. Annual reports published by Life Insurance Corporation Housing Finance (LICHF) was also used. The housing policy of the Central and State Governments, Several Five year plan documents and valuable literature from various libraries were used in this study.

Appropriate statistical tools were used to find out the efficient performance of LICHFL from the opinion of the beneficiaries and to study the validity of the hypothesis.

## CHAPTERISATION

The first chapter deals with the introduction, significance of the study, statement of the problem, period of study, objectives, hypotheses, methodology, limitations of the study and plan of the chapters.

The second chapter provides a review of literature available on the research topic.

The third chapter brings out the profile of the study area. It provides information about the population, health facilities and health administrative set up in the study area.

The fourth chapter describes the housing finance system and the housing finance policies in India and in Tamilnadu.

The fifth chapter traces the Operational and Financial performance of the LIC Housing Finance Limited.

The sixth chapter presents the impact of LIC Housing Finance Limited on its beneficiaries in Chennai City.

The final chapter summarizes the findings and conclusions of the study and offers suggestions for the improvement of the institution.

REVIEW OF LITERATURE

# CHAPTER II

## REVIEW OF LITERATURE

A brief account of available literature pertinent to the present study is presented in this chapter. The related literature works as guideline not only in regard to the quantum of work done in the field, but also enable us to perceive the gap in the concerned field of research. The review of related literature manifests the significance of the present research study and relevance of the variable chosen. The present study provides comparative data on the basis of analysis, interpretation and evaluating in order to justify the hypothesis formulated and to be tested. It is considered to be a variable process between earlier studies done and present study. In this review of literature relevant information from articles, books and websites has been included. This information has been grouped under the following categories:

1. Homelessness and Housing Problem
2. Trends in urbanization
3. Government participation in housing
4. Housing policy
5. Housing finance and investment
6. Institutions providing housing finance

# 1. HOMELESSNESS AND THE HOUSING PROBLEM

The United Nations Centre for Human Settlements, Nairobi[1] has pointed out that homelessness represents the most obvious and severe manifestation of the unfulfilment of the human right to adequate housing. While estimates on scale of homelessness are invariably difficult to ascertain with precision, it is generally mentioned in the relevant United Nations documents that there are about 100 million homeless persons in the world few, countries, if any have entirely eliminated homelessness and in many nations and further actions this phenomenon is clearly increasing rather than declining, and further action is clearly required to eradicate homelessness.

Cooper[2] defines 'Home' as "a very rich concept. He also states that it embodies ideas of comfort, belongingness, identity, security and others that are beyond the scope of this report. 'Home' may be defined as a place where a person is able to establish meaningful social relations with other through entertaining them in his/her own space or where the person is able to choose not to relate to others if that choice is made.

Caplow, Bahr, and Stevenberg[3] suggest the following definition of homelessness. "Homelessness is a condition of detachment from society characterized by the absence or attenuation of the affiliative bonds that link settled persons to a network of interconnected social structures."

---

[1] UNITED NATIONS CENTRE FOR HUMAN SETTLEMENTS (HABITAT), NAIROBI. **Strategies to combat homelessness**, (Series of publication in support of the global compaign for secure tenure to 03/2000), pp.2-3
[2] COOPER B., **Shadow people : the reality of homelessness in the 90's**, (paper presented Geographical-Archive, Reality-Australia on 14th June 1999).
[3] CAPLOW T, BAHR H.M, AND STEVENBERG D. **Homelessness**, (International Encyclopedia of the social sciences, Vol.6, Free Press New York), pp. 494-498

Daly[4] estimates that five people per thousand use emergency shelters in Canada. Combined with census figure, these give national estimates of 130-360,000 homeless people and the United States of America estimates give a very varied picture. About 1.5-2.5 people per thousand population are judged to the absolutely or temporarily homeless, i.e. users of public shelters.

Epstein[5] states through his studies that there was 2.5 million people homeless in the United States of America in 1991. He also added that the number got increased from 1980.

Raj and Baross[6] account that the housing shortage is taken as a measure of homelessness on the ground that, if a household must share someone else's living accommodation, or a dwelling is due for demolition, it is homelessness. If it is so India would probably have some 20 million homeless households (probably 110 million homeless people in total) on this measure alone. If such of those who are not sharing dwelling but have poor servicing and those whose tenure is very uncertain are added, the number will become very large indeed.

Charles Abrams[7] observes that despite man's unprecedented progress in industry, education, and the sciences, the simple refuge affording privacy and protection against the elements is still beyond the reach of most members of the

---

[4] DALY G, **Homeless Policy, Strategies and lives on the street, London and New York, Routledge.** (United Nations Centre for Human Settlements, Nairobi).
[5] EPSTEIN, **Dependency served: rhetorical assumptions governing the education of homeless children and youth,** (unpublished paper delivered at the International sociological Association, Midterm conference, Jerusalem, 1995), December 28
[6] RAJ M AND BAROSS P, **Missed opportunities for state intervention in urban housing: an open heart surgery on the housing need model,** (United Nation Centre for Human settlements Nairobi, Kenya, Open House International, Vol.15, No.4, 1990) pp. 19-23.
[7] CHARLES ABRAMS, **Housing in the modern world,** (Faber and Faber, London, 1966) p.1.

human race. The unevenness of man's advance from the lower species is best illustrated in his struggle for shelter.

The World Bank Paper[8] observes that housing has substantial social benefits including the welfare effects of shelter from the elements, sanitation facilities and access to health and education services. Improved health and education and better access to income-earning opportunities can lead to higher productivity and earnings for low-income families. It is thus for sound economic reasons that, after food, housing is typically the largest item of household expenditure for poor families, and that they are willing to go to great lengths to obtain housing at locations with access to employment even if this means incurring the risks of illegal 'squatting'.

Devandra B Gupta and Ashish Bose[9] points out that housing is unique among consumer goods in the degree to which it can enhance or diminish the well being of individuals and families. A house constitutes possibly the most expensive single item which individuals ever buy and except for food, expenditure on shelter takes the largest part of the budget of most family.

Sudhendhu Mukherjee[10] identifies that the ongoing shelter problem in the less developed countries is very critical as millions of people live without a roof over their head or many reside in squatter settlements without any basic amenities of life. The living conditions of the urban poor who are typically housed in slums are extremely poor and the conditions are not encouraging for a safe and human dignity. The bulk

---

[8] WORLD BANK, **Housing sector policy paper.** (Washington: World Bank, 1975), p.2.

[9] DEVENDRA B GUPTA AND ASHISH BOSE, **Housing Delhi's millions – A study of the rent structure 1958-73** (National Building Organisation and United Nations Regional Housing Centre, Government of India, New Delhi, Escap 1976), p.3.

[10] SUDHENDHU MUKHERJEE, **Who are these pavement dwellers,** (a paper presented at the regional congress of local authorities for development of human settlements in Asia and the pacific, Yokahama, Japan, 9-16 June 1982), p.1.

Bakshi D. Sinha[13] points out that the serious housing problem is faced due to effects of population. He also states that the situations of the cities is depressing and the prospects of providing the expanding population with adequate housing services and amenities are not bright and this situation is further aggravated by other factors such as inequitable income distribution, ethnic, caste and religious differences. The demand for increased housing facilities are sought to be met by concerted action on the part of Government and housing authorities.

Betrand Renaud[14] identifies housing finance problem as the need to reconcile three partially conflicting objectives: affordability for the households, viability for the financial institutions and resource mobilization for the expansion of the sector and the national economy.

Sazanami Hidehiko[15] states that as economies become increasingly consumer-oriented, feelings of economic inferiority become distressing more and more people. In the developed, free enterprise countries, innovations in ways of life come less from the spontaneous demands of people than from manufacturers eager to market new commodities, which further accentuate unbalanced standards of living. In developing countries, top priority is given to economic development while social development, including housing and city planning, is left far behind.

---

[13] BAKSHI D.SINHA, **Housing growth in India**, (Birla Institute of Scientific Research Economic Division, New Delhi) p.80
[14] BETRAND RENAUD, **Housing Microfinance**, (Edited by Franck Daphnis and Bruce Ferguson, Kumarian press Inc, 2004) p.1
[15] SAZANAMI HIDEHIKO, **Housing in Metropolitan Areas** in simon R. Miles (ed), Metropolitan problems (Toronto Methuen, 1970), pp. 127 & 128

Jorgarsen[16] studied the effective demand for housing and other factors such as market, price, rental value, location, appearance, infrastructural services and the availability of finance. He states that an important aspect of the demand for housing is often overlooked: it is income-inelastic, i.e., as family income rises, expenditure on housing does not increase proportionally. This is particularly true for the lowest income strata where demand for food and clothing is sometimes reduced below normally acceptable levels in order to secure a roof over one's head. But also at higher income levels housing demand is inelastic. To ignore this fact by defining "affordability" as 25-30 per cent of income, as is common policy in many institutions, is but doing injustice to the poor spend more than one fourth of their income on housing".

Chaurasiya[17] has suggested that an integrated plan approach should be followed to construct planned colonies for future development. Top priority in proper land use and planning was emphasized by him.

James R.Follain, Gill Chin Lim and Betrand Renaud[18] has suggested that needs and standards of adequacy should not taken into consideration while defining the housing demand.

Gopinath Rao[19] has analyzed the difficulties faced by the buyers of flat in not getting the proportionate undivided share of land, and as regards unreasonable

[16] JORGARSEN N.O, **Housing Finance for low income groups**, (2nd edition, Rotterdam, Bouwereterum, Housing Research and Development Unit, University of Nairobi, 1982), p.2
[17] CHAURASIA B.P, **Urban land use and planning**, (Clugh publication, Allahabad 1987), pp.102-111
[18] JAMES R. FOLLANIN, GILL CHIN LIM AND BETRAND RENAUD, **Housing crowding in developing countries and willingness to pay for additional space, the case study of Korea**, (WBRS 269,1932), pp. 249-255
[19] GOPINATH RAO C.H, **Need for amendment for laws to and Housing Development**, (The Hindu, 27th November 1992).

increase in rates, construction of building in violation of approved plans, delay in handing over the flats. Further, he is of the view that the formal sector contributes only to high income group and middle income group. He has suggested that the promoters should be registered with MMDA, which should take action against them in the event of their demanding high land price, shortage of space etc.

## 2. TRENDS IN URBANISATION

Stanley D. Brunn and Jack F. William[20] has identified urbanization as a process involving two phases namely the movement of people from rural to urban place where they engage in primarily non-rural functions of occupations and the change in their life style from rural to urban with its associated values, attitudes and behaviors. The important variable in the former are population density and economic functions whereas the latter depend on social, psychological and behavioral factors.

Hawley[21] identifies that the radical changes in industrial production, transportation and communication altered the dimensions of city and brought large scale urbanization in new heights.

Murukados[22] has studied that the pattern of urbanization in India does not exhibit much variations from other less developing countries. Much of the population pressure in the cities came from the rush of migrants from rural areas in search of

---

[20] STANLEY D. BRUNN AND JACK F.WILLIAMS, **Cities of the world regional urban development**, (Charper and Raw publishers, New York, 1983), p.5.
[21] HAWLEY A.H, World Urbanisation: **Trends and prospects. The population of the world, Voice of America and lectures**, (Study circle Reprint Higginbothams private limited, Madras, 1967), pp. 97-98
[22] MURUKADOS C, **Population growth and Economic development: analyses of Indian experience since 1950**, (Dissertation submitted to University of Madras for the M. Litt. degree in Economics, Unpublished, 1974), p. 250.

work, in urban centers. He has a view that these migrants are prepared for city life, nor the cities prepared to receive them and in most of the advanced countries the rural urban drift resulted primarily from increased labour requirements in industries in the cities and reduction in labour requirements in rural areas brought about by advance in agricultural production techniques. He also noted that the recent influx of migrants to the Indian cities occurred with almost no encouragement from industrial employment opportunities.

Khurana[23] described the housing scenario in India in urban and rural areas. The backlog of housing shortage had been increasing year after year due to low rate of dwelling construction in comparison to increase in households both in urban and rural areas. He also highlighted briefly the role of government and research development and extension agencies in housing development leading to construction and provision of affordable house to the people.

Nelson[24] points out that urbanization is not merely a way of thinking and behaving, but urbanized man, wherever he may be is ever adjusting to the new and changing as he is congenial to initiative, he may also be tolerant of tradition stands in the way of getting things done. He also identifies that urbanized man is not only mobile by himself, but he accepts the mobility of others and may be loyal to his immediate family but tends to lose contacts with other relatives.

---

[23] KHURANA M.L, **Housing development agencies**, (The Tamil Nadu Journal of co-operation, vol.82, no.1, April 1990).
[24] NELSON, **India's social transformation**, (Allied publishers private limited, New Delhi, 1979). p.62.

Victor[25] observes that urbanization has been one of the major forces of change in society and when it coupled with industrialization it brings about large scale and fundamental changes in the society. He also says that many of the aspects and problems of the societies of today become significant when viewed from the perspective of urbanization.

Narasimhalu[26] felt that people migrate to urban areas in search of high business in order to make huge money and wealth for themselves. He also adds that due to these increasing urbanization providing houses to all the people have become a serious problem, as rents are high in the urban areas.

Smita Sen gupta[27] felt that the immigration of the people to the core city from rural and other parts of the country makes the 'Housing problem' in the urban areas a big issue. As a result, people start moving towards adjoining suburban areas in order to get spacious and cheaper residential accommodations, which results in a 'Rapid sub urbanization.

## 3. GOVERNMENT PARTICIPATION IN HOUSING

The first five year plan[28] observes that during the plan period the State cannot afford to confine its role in this field to planning and regulation. It also identifies that the private enterprise is not in a position to do the job so far as low-income groups are

---

[25] VICTOR S.D SOUZA, **Urbanisation in India**, (Sage publications, 2003), p.31
[26] NARASIMHALU K, **Census 2001 and human development in India**, (Serials publications, 2004), p.19.
[27] SMITA SEN GUPTA, **Residential pattern of suburbs Delhi**, (concept publishing company, 1988), p.5.
[28] GOVERNMENT OF INDIA, **First five Year Plan**, p.598

concerned. They cannot afford to pay the economic rent for housing accommodation of even the minimum standards. The state has, therefore, to fill the gap and assist the construction of suitable houses for low and middle income groups both in urban and rural areas as part of its own functions. This would involve a large measure of assistance, which may take the form of subsidies on a generous scale and the supply of loans on a somewhat low rate of interest.

Fourth Five Year Plan document[29] observed that the experience of housing is that its unit cost are high and that with the constraint of resources it is not possible for public operations to touch even the fringe of the problem. Slum clearance schemes often lead to creation of new slums or deterioration of conditions in some of the older slums. In growing cities of a reasonable size, it should be part of government policy to encourage, through proper planning and land policy, adequate supply of housing. In cities where slum population is large, this approach would not be effective and it would be necessary to try to ameliorate the living conditions of slum dwellers as an immediate measure. Limiting the rise in the prices of land, providing financial assistance to co-operative and private effort and assuming legal powers for reconditioning of slums should be emphasized.

Rahul Srivastava[30] Observed that the Sixth Plan (1980-85) focused on integrated provision of services along with shelter, particularly for the poor. The Integrated Development of Small and Medium Towns (IDSMT) was launched in towns with population below 1 lakh for roads, pavements, minor civic works, bus-stands, markets, shopping complexes etc. Positive inducements were proposed for

---

[29] PLANNING COMMISSION, **Fourth Five Year plan**, p.402
[30] RAHUL SRIVASTAVA, **Planning the past**: History of India.

setting up new industries and commercial and professional establishments in small, medium and intermediate towns. Many of the 4,000-plus townships and urban agglomerations that are part of the 2001 census are a legacy of these moves.

Amid[31] points out that one of the basic principles enshrined in the constitution of India is to provide basic socio-economic necessities such as food, clothing and shelter. Consequently, since early fifties our five year plans were directed towards the aim of achieving the goals of providing the basic necessities to the teeming millions in the country.

Buckley, Dunham, Walk and Personal[32] observes that developing countries all over the world seem to have accepted the perspective of providing a range of support policies that go beyond direct provision of housing. They also expressed that in a similar vein the National housing policy advocated a facilitative role of public sector, rather than that of a housing producer and amongst a variety of policy instruments identified under the role, those related to housing finance are probably the most crucial.

Fifth plan document[33] emphasized the relation between the housing strategy and a well-formulated land policy. It points out that one of the main impediments in the way of increased housing activity is the non-availability of land at reasonable prices and it is an universal experience that if housing plots are available at reasonable prices, large sections of the community are willing to undergo considerable privation and inconvenience, in order to construct and own houses. It

[31] AMID, **The problem of Housing in developing countries,** (Proceedings of international association for housing science, vol.1. 1978), p.50.
[32] BUCKLEY R, DUNHAM C.R, WALKER J.C, AND PERSONAL T, **Private housing finances for low income households in India,** (Urban institutes, Washington. 1989), p.313.
[33] PLANNING COMMISSION, Draft Fifth Five Year Plan. p.261.

also states that a proper strategy for the housing sector cannot, therefore, be thought of in isolation and unrelated to well formulated land policy.

Seventh five year plan[34] observes that the time has come for the Government to set before itself a clear goal in the field of housing and launch a major housing effort, not so much to build but to promote housing activity through the supply of financial infrastructure such that every family will be provided with adequate shelter within a definite time horizon. It also felt that direct subsidy to urban housing should be avoided as far as possible and it should be small and be in the form of infrastructure facilities so as not to create large differences between the market values and subsidized prices.

Sharp Evelyn[35] points out that the beginning of governmental interest in housing can be traced back to the 19th century when the problem of sanitation and control over disease began to impress themselves upon the national conscience. He also added that sanitation and housing were regarded as twin problems which oppressed the homeless poor.

The Planning Commission[36] points out that in a purely economic approach housing needs could be formulated in terms of effective demand of households for housing specifically large sectors of the population in India are not only inadequately housed but also are without sufficient economic resources to improve their housing

[34] PLANNING COMMISSION, **The Seventh Five Year Plan**, p.293.

[35] SHARP EVELYN, **The Ministry of housing and local government.** (George allen and unwin Limited, London, 1969), p.69.

[36] PLANNING COMMISSION, **Housing needs and Demand projections of housing in Tamil Nadu upto 1991.** (1982), pp.1-6.

situation, the needs of these sectors therefore could not be considered effective demand for housing.

Chris Paris[37] observed that governments have an enormously varied menu of housing policy options which can stimulate housing construction through direct subsidies or tax concessions to builders or enhancing the relative attraction of investment in housing compared with other investment items.

Sixth five year plan[38] stated that in view of the constraints on public resources, there should be greater encouragement of the private sector to step up its activities in the construction of housing for low and middle income groups. It also points out that imaginative schemes of improved facilities for financial intermediation in this sector will have to be investigated in order to achieve this objective.

Renu S. Karnad[39] states that in the past, most South Asian governments viewed housing as a social rather than an economic sector. For these governments, housing and subsidies were synonymous and hence the tendency was to view housing finance from the angle of its cash budget and not as a developmental activity with tremendous spin-offs to the economy. Today, this has clearly changed. The most significant step taken by the governments has been the fostering of 'public-private partnerships'. He also points out that governments appear to have recognized that monopolistic state owned providers of housing finance are not be the most efficient or cost effective mechanism to develop and deepen the mortgage market. Merits of

---

[37] CHRIS PARIS, **Housing Australia**, (Macmillan education, Australia PTY Limited, 1993), p.56.
[38] SIXTH FIVE YEAR PLAN, **Planning Commission**, (Government of India 1980-85), p.389.
[39] RENU, S KARNAD, **Housing finance and the economy: Regional trends South Asia: perspectives**, (The 25th World Congress international union for housing finance June 23, 2004), p.3.

private sector dedicated housing finance institutions have been recognized and encouraged.

Chitharanjan[40] has discussed the problem of three aspects namely urban employment, declaration of housing as economic sector and economic implications of housing. He has emphasized recognition of housing as an economic sector and he was in favour of devising policy measures for tapping employment potentials of the housing.

## 4. HOUSING POLICY

Dattarai[41] has observed that the Government intervention in the housing sector received special care and attention during the late 1960's when housing boards in almost all states and the slum clearance boards in certain states were established in India and the formulation of the National housing policy by the Ministry of Urban Development is termed as a landmark in the history of India's housing policy.

Ford Krishna[42] points out that housing policy is an essential weapon in the city's struggle to maintain and perpetuate itself, to provide an attractive living environment which enhance the accomplishment and aspirations of its inhabitants, which provides a tax base and a business environment that will sustain and increase the changes of meaningful livelihood for all of its people.

Choudhri[43] described that the execution of housing policies is trusted with the state governments and its financial burden is partly borne by the central government

---

[40] CHITHARANJAN K.V, **Broader Economic perspectives of urban housing**, (Nagarlok, vol.18, January - March 1986), pp. 1-9.
[41] DATTARAI G, **Metro issues – case study of Madras**, (MMDA, May 1988), p.3
[42] FORD KRISHNA, Housing policy and the urban middle class, (Transaction books, New Jercy, 1978), p. XXXI.
[43] CHOUDHRI INDRAJIT, **Public policy for urban shelter: The Indian Scenario**, (Nagarlok, vol.XIX Oct-Dec 1987), p.21.

and moreover the state governments are vested with powers to pursue specific housing Programmes in adherence with the socio-economic and political situation. He also points out that the formulation and execution of housing policies in Madras Metropolitan area also have its bearings in lines with the policy pursuance of the state and central government.

Duncan Meclan[44] studied the overall conduct of Government policy for housing in Britain. He has analysed the factors influencing the housing demand and supply. Price and income elasticity are classified by him as the factors responsible for the changes in the demand for housing. Employment and business are the two factors influencing the supply for housing.

Aravindhakshan[45] has studied the housing plan proposed by the Government of India. He said that housing is not only a basic necessity of human living but also a vital sector of the economy. He has classified difficulties in the planning of housing into Organisational difficulties, Financial difficulties and Social difficulties. He has identified the causes for these three kinds of problems and suggested that the housing plan also can be implemented through IRDP schemes. He has suggested that a careful implementation of the schemes alone will be useful to

overcome the above said difficulties. Further, he has suggested that the monetary agencies must have a wide network and must have continuous to the officials. Also there must be constant supervision and direction.

[44] DUNCLAN MACLEN, **Housing Economics**, (Longman group Limited, London, 1982), pp. 36- 76.
[45] AARAVINDHAKSHAN, K, **A New housing policy for India**, (1981), pp. 12-62.

Jayaram and Sandhur[46] have studied the policy and perspective of housing in India. They have elaborately discussed the housing problem in India and provided a critique of the policy measures so far undertaken. They have suggested development of cooperative housing and expansion of housing by utilizing the available undeveloped land. They have also said that a realistic housing policy has to be formulated on the interrelated issues of housing finance, land ceiling, slum improvement, rent control and housing technology.

Khodaiji[47] has stated that migration of rural population into urban areas would aggravate the housing problem in cities. He has suggested that proper policy should be evolved aiming at the optimum utilization of the resources necessary for housing.

Shapire[48] studies that the development of policy in the housing finance sector should allow more competition in financial markets, with households gaining greater variety of housing finance services with lower risk and lower cost.

## 5. HOUSING FINANCE AND INVESTMENT

The Housing Finance Manual[49] designed for developing countries while targeting the group defines to whom the housing finance strategy is intended and made accessible. It defines...

---

[46] JAYARAM, N. AND SANDHU R.S, **Housing in India problems, policy and perspectives**, (B.R. Publishing corporation, New Delhi, 1984), pp. 25-35.

[47] KHODAIJI, B.J, **Today in the context of tomorrow-Housing scheme**, (civic affairs, December 1987), pp. 102-117

[48] SHAPIRE M.S., **The urban edge issues and innovations**, (The John hoplairs university press, U.S.A., 1988), p. 4.

[49] HOUSING FINANCE MANUAL FOR DEVELOPING COUNTRIES, **A Methodology for Designing housing finance institutions center for human settlements**, (Habitat, Nairobi, 1991), p.17.

"Housing Finance is the capital made available to a household to improve or acquire a house. Acquiring a house might mean building a house or buying one that has been built by someone else. The house might be bought from any of a number of sources, including the builder, another household or, even, a landlord, and the seller may be an individual or institution. The amount of housing finance required will depend primarily on the gap between the cost of acquisition and the amount already available to the purchaser. However, demand can only become effective, if the household is able and willing to borrow the amount. Its ability to borrow will depend on the terms of the loan as well as its own financial circumstances. Its willingness is likely to depend upon regarding the value of the house or improvements."

Francis Cherunilam & Odeyar D. Heggade[50] pointed out that, financing housing is an important element of housing policies pursued by the Governments of developed and developing countries of the world in the post world war years. The financial markets in housing are comparatively well-developed in advanced countries but they are in their infancy in the Third world countries.

REDCLIFF Committee[51] has observed that credit availability, rather than the rate of interest, is the more important determinant of investment in long term assets like housing. The Committee also considers credit availability to be crucial for financing construction, additions to stocks and other regular items of expenditure.

---

[50] FRANCIS CHERUNILAM & ODEYAR .D HEGGADE. **Housing in India**, (Himalaya publishing house), p.105
[51] REPORT OF THE COMMITTEE ON WORKING ON MONETARY SYSTEM. **London HMSO**, (1959), p.132.

Cedric Pugh[52] in his text discusses and indicates the following upon Housing Finance and its potentials as:

First, the housing capital market and Government stand as intermediaries between the production-consumption process in the economy on one hand and the housing system on the other.

Second, housing systems in the developing countries are inequitous, reflecting the prior inequality in the ownership of capital and earnings from work in the production-consumption economy. In countries such as India the inequality will be very conspicuous, with contrasts between life in a villa, in a leafy suburb and life on a city pavement.

Third, urban development creates assets, which in total represent enormous economic and social value. From the reformist view, we can perceive the potentials here to add to urban investments, and to use housing policy as a means of extending property rights, to households in the income range below the eightieth percentile. Households above the eightieth percentile will be able to exercise their housing choices, largely without Government economic assistance or incentives.

Fourth, some of the thrust in the foregoing three points is towards spreading the extent of owner-occupied housing and land. In this fourth point we add some cautions circumspection. Housing and land policies have to be coordinated to ensure that land price escalation is curbed. If they are not coordinated in such a way that abundant supplies of housing and affordable land are forthcoming, various economic problems will arise.

---

[52] CEDRIC PUGH, **Housing and Urbanisation**, (Chapter III, Housing finance, The Economy and housing welfare, Sage publications), pp. 72 & 73.

John G. Gurley and Edward S. Shaw[53] analyze the Housing Finance System and the economy through size, scope and efficiency. They narrate that it is difficult to attain a satisfactory rate of growth in real output. Such a growth rate may not be achieved for a number of reasons, some social, some psychological, some political and some economic. What is significant here is that the rudimentary economy places severe financial restraints on the growth of real output. And immature financial system is in itself an obstacle to economic progress.

Lal A.K[54]. says that the informal sector, on the other hand, contributes to the housing finance system through various sources which include sale of personal assets such as personal savings in cash and kind, sale of personal assets such as jewellery, land and agricultural property, and borrowings from friends, relatives and informal money lenders/credit unions.

Murukadas C[55] observes the need for investment in housing is one of the most important factors determining how effectively a nation's investment can be made in raising productivity. The proportion of resources going into such investments exert a major influence on the capital co-efficient for the whole economy.

Coale A.J and Hoover E.M[56] points out that an economy in which investment in housing is high would clearly tend to have a higher capital output ratio. It may not be incorrect to say that adequate housing may have an important role in affecting the attitudes, health and efficiency of the labour force poor and crowded housing in the

---

[53] JOHN G. GURLEY AND EDWARDS. SHAW, **Money in a theory of finance**, (The Brooking institutions, Washington, D.C, 1980), p.46.
[54] LAL A.K, **Handbook of low cost housing**, (New Age International private limited publishers, Daryaganj, New Delhi), p.7.
[55] MURUKADAS C., **op.cit**, p. 26
[56] COALE A.J AND HOOVER M., **Population growth and Economic development in low income countries** (Princeton University press-princeton, 1958), p.32.

slums of rapidly growing towns and cities certainly retard the efficiency of the labour force. Hence the provision for investment in housing can, in a way, be regarded as a form of investment in human resources. Consequently housing and other similar investments occupy a hybrid or intermediate position in regard to economic development.

Paul F.Wendt[57] points out that investment in housing may be enhanced considerably by extending tax reliefs on such investments and these tax relief measures have succeeded in diverting more personal and corporate money to investments in housing.

Devendra B. Gupta, Sanat Kaul & Rita Pandey[58] observed that a salient feature of financial intermediation in India is the government presence and control. They also identifies that Indian government through its various policies, including fiscal and monetary, and regulation, is able to influence directly and indirectly the flow of funds into the housing finance sector.

Mathur G.C[59] observed that the relative economics of a repair programme vis-a vis new construction is the relative real cost involved in rehabilitating existing stock as against creating new stock and new housing construction requires huge investment to create educational, medical, transport, and recreational services along with new housing. He also points out that repaired houses do not call for fresh investments since such facilities are already available on purely economic considerations and

[57] PAUL F. WENDT, **Housing Policy**, (Berkeley and Los Angeles: University of Californial press, 1966), p. 134.
[58] DEVENDRA B. GUPTA, SANAT KAUL AND RITA PANDEY, **Housing and India's Urban poor**, (Har-Anand Publications, 1993), p.118.
[59] MATHUR G.C, **Conservation of Existing housing stock**, (Nagarlok, Oct-Dec. 1979), p.68.

therefore, a housing preservation programme is beneficial and prevents premature depletion of housing sock by obsolescence.

Mare Myers .J[60] says that as an investment the housing decision requires studies on proper financing for it. He also points out that the source of finance may be either owned or externally borrowed but the combination of the two may be attempted at a proper mix to maximize overall return on total wealth.

Baswaraja .M and Gowrappa .K[61] in their article stated that investment in housing was not accorded due priority in the programme of planned development and the continuous neglect of this sector had made the housing problem colossal both in urban and rural India. The article analyse the sources of housing finance, both formal and informal. The authors also compared the interest rates charged by different housing finance institutions such as NHB, HDFC, and CANFIN for different loan amount.

Samentak Das[62] analysed the total investment in housing under the five year plans. He added that in India the flow of credit into the housing sector came from two sources, the formal sector and the informal sector. He concluded that Government should concentrate on upgradation and improving the facilities are creating an enabling environment for housing finance activities by eliminating constraints.

---

[60] MARE MYERS .J, **Complete guide to investment opportunities**, (Macmillan Co., New York, 1982), p. 711.
[61] BASWARAJA .M AND GOWRAPPA .K, **Housing finance in India**, (Journal of accounting and finance, vol.VI, No.2. 1992).
[62] SAMENTAK DAS, **Housing finance-some relevant issues**, (The Journal of Management accountant, December 1996).

Ramanujam S.R.[63] observes that investments in the housing sector have an multiplier effect on industry and employment and the importance of the housing sector can be judged from the estimate that for every rupee invested in the construction of houses, 78 paise gets added to the gross domestic product of India, also the real estate sector is subservient to the development of 269 other industries.

Mutalib M.A. and Mohamed Akbar Ali Khan[64] points out that central financial assistance is being given to states in the form of 'Block grants' for all the state sector schemes including housing schemes and the State governments are free to utilize the central assistance on any state plan scheme according to their own requirements and priorities.

Larry S.Bourne[65] states that there are at least three distinct levels which must be differentiated in examining the sources of housing finance; first, the national level, involving the allocation of capital to the housing sector as part of aggregate capital markets; second, the firm level, at which capital is allocated to the producers and institutions which finance housing and third the provision of capital to consumers.

Katuri Nageswara Rao[66] states that housing finance has prospered through the innovative application of technology. He also points out that many nations have been encouraging private sector initiatives in housing finance with a view to meet the ever growing demand and there are tax shelters for the borrowers. The author also felt that lending institutions have been generally operating under conditions of financial

[63] RAMANUJAM S.R, Indian **infrastructure**, (Vol. Issue 8, March 2006), p. 119.
[64] MUTALIB M.A AND MOHAMED AKBAR ALI KHAN, **Ed. Public Housing**, (Sterling publishers, NewDelhi, 1986) p.5.
[65] LARRY S. BOURNE, **The Geography of housing**, (Edward Arnold Publishers Limited, London, 1981), p.117.
[66] KATURI NAGESWARA RAO, **Housing finance-global perspective**, (Professional Banker, June 2006), p. 1.

stability with accent on rational loan pricing, relying essentially on credit scoring models.

Mulkh Raj[67] observed that a study noted that only 22 per cent of the total housing investments in the India during 1982-83 were met by the funds extended under the formal arrangements which includes the five year plan allocations, allocations for housing in 'Revenue Budgets' of the Central, State Governments, loans extended by the general financial institutions such as LIC, commercial banks, deposits mobilizations by the housing cooperatives, investments by the public sector and private sector specialized housing agencies, employers loans to their staff for house building and the rest 78 percent of the housing investments were met by the funds mobilized through informal arrangements.

Jayshree Vyas[68] points out that housing finance should not be seen in isolation but it should be linked with commercial loans for working capital and with equipment term loans. She also added that attention must move from trying to turn the poor and women into mere users of housing finance to becoming owners of housing finance institutions and there is a need for linking housing finance with other private, public and government housing schemes.

Assocham Recommendations[69] observed that the central issue in home financing is affordability and absence of sound mortgage finance coupled with high interest rates for long-term loans are hindering development of housing. It also added

---

[67] MULKH RAJ, **The world bank staff working papers** (No.658, Washington, World bank, 1984), p.4.

[68] JAYSHREE VYAS, **Financing shelter and housing for poor women in India**, (Office of Development studies, Bureau for Development policy, United Nations Development Programme), p. .9.

[69] ASSOCHAM RECOMMENDATIONS, **India Competing for the future**, (New Delhi), pp. 19-21.

that to increase demand for housing, easy availability of loans at low interest rates is essential to enable buyers purchase homes at the beginning of careers and such long term loans should be based on primary mortgages backed by government insurance and guarantee programmes.

Sanjiv Shankaran[70] points out that to find out if the housing finance business will grow at a high rate in the next few years, it is necessary to study the factors that spurred the growth. Housing finance received a boost through a combination of growing demand and rising affordability. While the demand for housing has always been there and will be for a long time to come, its increased affordability was the real key to growth.

Bijlani H.U[71] observes that mortgage insurance has attract institutional, large individual investors who seek a higher return than provided by saving account and who otherwise would invest outside of home financing field.

The Editorial of the Economic times[72] observed that monetary policies influence the availability of housing finance. Lack of development of grass-roots financial institutions means a lack of mortgage funds. Similarly fiscal policies are critical to a country's ability to mobilize resources from growth and the distribution of income. It also highlights the countries with a poorly conceived overall policy framework cannot expect to deal effectively with their housing problems. All these apply in some measure or the other to our own country. The Estimates committee in a report some time ago regretted that even after 25 years of independence, the

---

[70] SANJIV SHANKARAN, **Business line**, (financial daily in "The Hindu", April 28, 2003).
[71] BIJLANI H.U, **Housing finance, mortgage insurance and secondary mortgage markets**, (Nagarlok, vol.XI, No.4, IIPA, New Delhi, Oct-Dec 1979), p.72.
[72] EDITORIAL, **Housing problem**, (The Economic Times, 26th May 1979).

government has not been able to evolve a national policy on housing. That in respect of basic necessity like providing shelter to the common man, successive five-year plans have virtually abdicated their function, no matter what the excuses are, cannot glossed over.

Devendra B.Gupta[73] has studied the details relating to investment in housing in India both private and public and proportionate contribution of the housing industry to the overall employment position. He has recommended that the attitude of the people should change. They must be motivated to invest in housing rather than in gold and gold ornaments.

Renauld Betrand[74] has made a study of the housing and financial institutions in developing countries. He has identified that the weak existence of borrowed capital in the developing countries is the main cause for the inadequate development of housing financial development. He has concluded saying that the problem of housing finance could be solved only through reconciling three conflicting objectives: improve competitions, increase efficiency and stimulate long term finance.

Sharma K.S.R.N[75] has analysed certain specific issues of housing finance in India. The first issue raised by him is that the NHB failed to take the initative in the mobilization of funds by encouraging the enlightened elite groups to deposit their additional savings with them. For that purpose he suggested that a saving linked housing schemes should be developed. Further, he has suggested that fiscal concessions and incentives should be given in order to attract the savings of the

[73] DEVENDRA .B GUPTA, **Urban housing in India**, (World Bank staff paper, No.730), pp 1-73.
[74] RENAULD BETRAND, **Housing and financial institutions in Developing countries**, (World Bank staff paper No.658, 1983), pp. 100 – 104.
[75] SHARMA K.S.R.N, **Housing finance in India**, (Indian Institution of Public Administration, New Delhi, 1989), pp.43-57.

public towards housing finance institutions. Fiscal and other incentives should be provided to the builders for construction of houses so as to encourage them to construct low cost houses and to provide inputs needed for house construction at a subsidy. In order to prevent default in the repayment of loan by the borrowers, he has suggested reliable administrative machinery and field agencies by which to recover the loans promptly.

Ramachandran P and Deodhar[76] have discussed the problems of housing investment in India in terms of monetary and fiscal aspects. Interest rate and deposits are analysed under the monetary aspects and taxes levied on housing income, property tax and wealth tax are analysed under the fiscal aspects. They have also recommended low cost housing schemes and the co-ordination between housing finance institutions and the money market.

The National Building Organisation[77] has discussed in the year 1982 certain aspects of demand for housing in India. It has analysed the trend in housing investment and the trend in housing stock.

Chetan Vaidhya[78] has analysed the income distribution and consumption patterns facilitating housing demand. Also he has analysed the existing demand for housing in Madras. He has suggested the increase of the supply of Housing finance also.

---

[76] RAMACHANDRAN P. AND DEODHAR, **Monetary and Fiscal Policies and Investment in India**, (Soumiya Publication Private Limited, Bombay, 1979), pp.49-58.
[77] NATIONAL BUILDING ORGANISATION, **The Economic Times in India**, (1982), pp. 65-83.
[78] CHETAN VAIDHYA, **Estimation of Demand for Housing Finance in Madras Urban India**, pp. 102-117.

## 6. INSTITUTIONS PROVIDING HOUSING FINANCE

The Chairman-cum-Managing Director of RBI, GUPTA P.K[79] feels that the consolidation of housing finance sector has happened to some extent, thanks to integration among housing finance companies. Banks, which currently hold a major chunk of the housing finance market, have tried hard to increase their penetration on this front. The number of housing finance companies, the ones that do only this business and little else, has reduced. Banks are developing fresh delivery channels and tapping new clients.

Acharya K.T.V[80] observes that open market borrowings are concerned, in view of the various difficulties involved in raising funds without a Government guarantee such as non-availability of specific securities to be offered, continuously increasing interest rates for deposits, etc., tight money market conditions in the country, HUDCO has been able to raise funds through market borrowings, i.e. by the issue of debenture bonds mainly on the basis of Government guarantee.

Prasad N.K[81] points that the Housing and Urban Development Corporation does not undertake housing construction directly by itself, rather it provides financial assistance to agencies directly involved in residential construction like State Housing Boards, City Improvement Trust Boards, Urban Development Authorities, Municipal Corporations and other institutions. He also states that these agencies formulate their own housing and site and services plans (land development plan) for financial assistance on soft terms to HUDCO.

---

[79] GUPTA P.K, **The Hindu, Business line,** (Friday, January 27, 2006).
[80] ACHARYA K.T.V. **HUDCO, A New Dimensions in Social Housing Financing.** (Nagarlok, Vol.XIII, No.3, IIPA, New Delhi, July-Sept. 1981), p. 80
[81] PRASAD N.K. **Housing and Urban Development – Role of HUDCO on National scale,** (Nagarlok, Vol.X, No.1, IIPA, New Delhi, Jan-Mar, 1978), p.34.

Moitra M.K[82] states that the Central Finance Ministry has to decide on the quantum of loan from LIC and the GIC to be earmarked for the socially oriented sectors, which include housing amongst other things. He also points out that this is a part of the plan resources, its allocation is decided by the Planning commission in consultation with the states, as a part of state's annual plan on a year-to-year basis.

Deepak Parekh[83] states that almost all Governments, with differing political persuasions, in the developing and the developed countries, had a similar objective for their citizens namely, to ensure that all families had decent house in a suitable living environment. The author highlighted the institutions that provided housing finance such as HUDCO, HDFC and Housing building advance to employees. He further suggested some policy measures for a future strategy with some key elements. He concluded that the sound structure of institutions would prove to have the most living impact, as the real development of housing activity in developing economics.

Verma R.V[84] outlined the institutions that extended the housing loan and concluded that there were wide gaps in the existing housing finance system and even the resources of all the institutions taken together would be grossly inadequate.

Vidyavathi .K[85] observed that in the developed world, most of the housing is financed through formal housing finance institutions, in developing countries like India, the extent of formal housing finance is quite limited. She also points out that the liberalization and the active entry of commercial banks into housing finance

---

[82] MOITRA M.K, **Housing and Urban Federalism**, (Nagarlok, Ocy-Dec 1982), p. 78.
[83] DEEPAK PAREKH, **Services marketing, The Indian experience**, (Marias Publications, Delhi, 1993).
[84] VERMA R.V. **Housing finance system, the emerging scenario**, (monthly commentary, December 1995).
[85] VIDYAVATHI K, **Role of Urban housing finance institutions in Karnataka**, (Finance India, Vol.XVI No.1, March 2002), pp 242-246.

market, deregulation of interest rate etc. increased the competition and affected the volume of housing companies.

The Shah committee[86] recommended, wherever possible, particularly for housing projects involving large amounts of money, consortium approach may be adopted involving commercial banks, HUDCO, Housing boards. LIC and other bodies, depending upon the nature of the schemes. In such consortium lending, repayment period in the case of banks may be fixed at more than 10 years, which can be longer for other general agencies.

Munjee Nasser .M[87] observes that there is no reason why a housing finance institution cannot be set up which encourages savings specifically for the purpose of housing. Its liabilities could be in the form of equity, long-term borrowing and deposits from the public, whereas its assess can be in the form of mortgage and direct housing investment. Further, such, an institution could attract short-term funds upto one year and use them to lend for longer periods. In other words, it would be operating on different points on the yield curve. Such a scheme would necessitate a lender of last resort facility from the Reserve Bank or a consortium of banks at a prefixed penalty rate in case of unforeseen withdrawals. Its operational feasibility would be much enhanced by the active existence of a secondary mortgage market.

---

[86] SHAH COMMITTEE, **Summary of the recommendations**, (which appeared in the records and statistics, 8th February, 1980).
[87] MUNJEE NASSER .M. **Housing Finance: Need for Reform**? (The Economic Times, 25th July 1978).

Giriappa .S[88] explains that the Constructions firms and building societies have become major institutions in housing system specializing in housing finance market. Apart from commercial banks, insurance companies, local authorities and other finance institutions and building societies have been increasing significantly in recent years. Their share has been more than 90 percent in many developed countries. In the developing countries however, their role has been hitherto somewhat handicapped. While being freely competitive the housing market may exhibit some monopoly or scarcity conditions during recession and times of emergencies.

Malhotra R.N[89] narrated the institution and non-institutional sources for housing activities. He also briefly mentioned the important principles essential for a sound housing finance company. He concluded that a well-managed housing finance institution could expect not only to serve a suitable social objective of helping people to procure shelter but also to earn reasonable profits.

Various literature presented in this chapter brings out enough scope for the present research work. The literature on housing problem has analysed the problems faced by the purchaser of house in getting finance. It also has been highlighted in the literature that the important aspect of the demand for housing is income-inelastic. It has been pointed that the immigration of the people to the main city from rural parts of the country makes the housing problem a big issue. The literature relating to the study has observed that the government participation in the housing sector by formulating the national housing policy is termed as important landmark in the history of housing policy. The above mentioned literature relating to housing finance

[88] GIRIAPPA .S. **Housing Finance and Development in India**, (Mohit Publications, New Delhi, 1998).

[89] MALHOTRA R.N. **Housing Finance**, (Reserve bank of India Bulletin, January 1991).

and investment viewed that the investments in the housing sector have an multiplier effect on industry and employment and concluded with the importance of institutions in providing housing finance. The profile of Chennai city, the study area of this research work is furnished in the next chapter.

# A PROFILE OF THE STUDY AREA

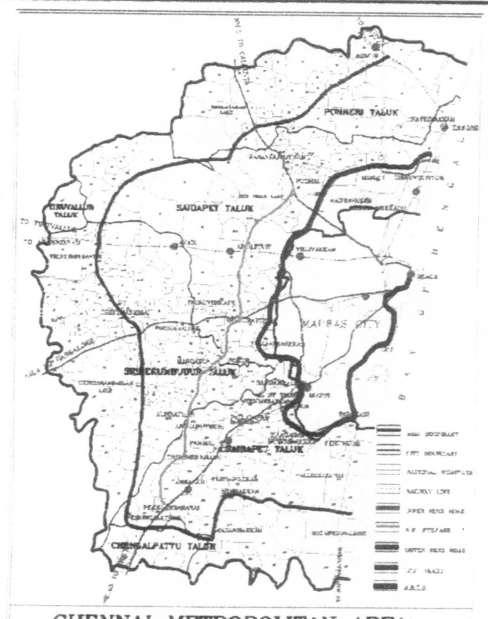

# CHENNAI METROPOLITAN AREA

# CHAPTER III

## A PROFILE OF THE STUDY AREA

This chapter deals with the profile of Chennai City, which is the study area for the purpose of this research. It traces the history of Chennai City, gives a brief presentation of its Geographical and physical background such as location and spread, climate and rainfall in the city. It highlights the Administrative divisions, culture and life styles and the demographic background of the city. Besides this, the amenities available in Chennai City like educational facilities, medical facilities etc. are also discussed. Housing development of the Chennai City is also discussed in this Chapter. As a prelude to the analysis of the primary data collected, a general profile of Chennai City is presented in this chapter as a preliminary step.

*This Chapter is presented under six different heads. They are:*

1. Evolution of Chennai City

2. Geographical and physical background

3. General profile of Chennai City

4. Demographic background

5. Infrastructural facilities and amenities

6. Housing development in Chennai City

# 1. EVOLUTION OF CHENNAI

Chennai is the capital of Tamil Nadu State and the gateway to Southern India. It is the Fourth largest metropolis in India next to Mumbai, New Delhi and Kolkatta. It has been playing an important role in the socio cultural and intellectual development of India. It was established in 1639 by East India Company of Britain as the chief trading center. Over the last 360 years, Chennai has evolved from a group of fishing hamlets and villages into the administrative and commercial center of the Madras Presidency during the colonial period, and the capital of the State of Tamilnadu after Independence.

The origin of the Chennai was from a small fishing village called Chennapatna located on the Cholamandalam Coast of Tamil Nadu in the vicinity of present fort area where the secretariat of the state government of Tamilnadu is located. The 5 square kilometer (Approximately) sand strip has now expanded into a 170 square kilometers Metropolis with the population of more than 6 million. Each of the scattered settlements separated by long distances grew around a temple, supported by irrigation tanks and their paddy fields. Purusawalkam, Mylapore, Thiruvallikeni, Thiruvatteeswaranpettai, Egmore, Nungambakkam and Saidapet are some of the well-known settlements. Starting with the nucleus of the fort, the city gradually grew incorporating old settlements and villages like Royapuram, Chintadripet, Thiruvallikeni and Purusawalkam. Fort area, a residential zone in the beginning, had become a commercial zone quickly during the initial period of the East India Company, and it has been a commercial area even today.

The earlier residential rings comprising Nungambakkam, Egmore and Kilpauk in the west, and Mylapore and Adyar in the South were the areas in which the British built their 'Garden houses'. These areas are also changing character from areas of single-family residential houses and bungalows to one of multifamily apartments and commercial complexes. The "Central Business District" (CBD) has moved southwards from George Town to the commercial areas ringing Anna Salai, Nungambakkam and Teynampet. The new residential development has been taking place towards the south and west in an ever-growing semi-circle with the CBD gradually moving southward.

Chennai City now spreads over an area of about 174 square kilometers, and the urban agglomeration is spreads over 531 square kilometers including the city and a number of major towns and panchayats. Chennai Metropolitan Area (CMA) encompasses the city, 5 Municipal councils, 5 townships, 26 town panchayats and a large number of rural settlements measuring over 1170 square kilometers, which is more than six times larger than city area.

## 2. GEOGRAPHICAL AND PHYSICAL BACKGROUND
## LOCATION AND SPREAD

Chennai is a low-lying area and the land surface is almost flat like a pancake. The even topography of the land throughout the district renders sub-divisions into natural regions rather difficult. It rises slightly as the distance from the seashore increases but the average elevation of the city is not more than 22' above mean sea level while most of the localities are just at sea level and drainage in such areas remain a serious problem. From very early times, Chennai was known for its pleasant scenery and was said to be a town open to sky and full of garden of mangoes, coconuts, guavas, oranges, etc.

Chennai, the coastal city is situated in the North East of Tamil Nadu along the coast of Bay of Bengal. The latitudes and longitudes are 13.6' North and 80.18'east respectively. It is bordered by the Bay of Bengal in the east, while the state of Andhra Pradesh is on its Northwest, Kerala and Karnataka in the western side. The City extends over an area of 43 kilometers from North to South and 29 kilometers East to West.

The East India Company made up their first settlement on a small sandy mould on an area of about 7 square kilometers presently occupied by Fort St. George. The Company thereafter acquired the scattered areas around Fort St. George in stages. Triplicane was the first to be acquired in 1676. The villages of Egmore, Purusawalkam and Tondiarpet were acquired in 1693. By 1708, the Company came into the possession of Tiruvottiyur, Nungambakkam, Vyasarpadi, Kathivakkam and Sathangadu. The Villages of vepery, Perimet and Perambur were added to their possession from the Nawab of Carnatic in the year 1742. Slowly the activities started increasing which resulted in enlarging the area to an extent of 70 square kilometers. The construction of harbour in 1881 and the laying of trunk Railway lines in 1856 and construction of major highways radiating from it, linking major cities of India have strengthened it to a pre-eminent position. In 1931, the present Mambalam area was annexed to the city, which took the city area to 75 square kilometers. In the next 40 years i.e. by 1971, Adyar, Guindy, Saidapet in the South and West Mambalam, Kodambakkam, Aminjikarai and Ayanavaram in the west were added to the city fold whose extent rose to 128 square kilometers. The new neighbourhoods like Annanagar and K.K.Nagar and ancient villages namely Velachery, Thiruvanmiyur and Erukancheri were added to the city, which had contributed to the rapid expansion of the city. Even now the adjoining areas around the city border claim to be included into the city area and, are classified as urban agglomeration area. Not withstanding this, the impact of the city in the nearby areas has been tremendous and their growth is also in tune with the city. Because of the high growth rate, the adjoining and the nearby areas have been grouped to form the Chennai Metropolitan Area extending from Ennore in the North, Perungalathur in the South and Poonamalle in the west totaling about 1177 square kilometers.

The growth of Chennai city and Metropolitan area are given in the Table 3.1.

### Table 3.1
### Growth of Chennai City and Metropolitan Area
(In square kilometers)

| Year | City Area | Metropolitan Area |
|------|-----------|-------------------|
| 1639 | 7.00 | - |
| 1871 | 70.00 | - |
| 1901-31 | 68.17 | - |
| 1941 | 77.24 | - |
| 1951 | 128.83 | - |
| 1961 | 128.83 | 1177.00 |
| 1971 | 128.83 | 1177.00 |
| 1981 | 172.00 | 1177.00 |
| 1991 | 172.00 | 1177.00 |
| 2001 | 172.00 | 1177.00 |

**Source: CMDA Reports**

## CLIMATE

Being situated in the tropical zone, Chennai normally has a very hot and humid climate. It has long summers and very short winter, after the period of North

East Monsoon seasons from October to December. The winter months of November to February are moderately cold with maximum temperature of 32°C and minimum temperature of 20°C and the summer months of April to June with a maximum of 40°C and minimum of 26°C are generally very hot and humid. The mean temperatures during the four quarters of the year are tabulated in Table 3.2.

**Table 3.2.**
**Chennai: Mean Temperatures**

| Season | Maximum | Minimum |
|---|---|---|
| January-March | 29-33° C | 20-24° C |
| April-June | 35-40° C | 26-28° C |
| July- September | 34-35° C | 25-26° C |
| October-December | 28-34° C | 21-25° C |

Chennai gets annual quota of rain mostly from Northeast Monsoon i.e. from October to December. Occasionally rain will start from later part of Southwest Monsoon. The tanks, which supply drinking water to the people of Chennai City, get water from catchment areas during this rainy season. The city gets a normal rainfall of 126 cms annually with a maximum of 76 cms during Northeast monsoon. Rain is minimum during winter months (January-February) and hot weather months (March to May).

## LANDUSE: PAST AND PRESENT

Chennai has been steadily growing in its importance in all aspects covering administration, higher education, specialized medical care, trade, commerce and industry. The Municipal Corporation of Chennai City had been generally controlling the pattern of development of area till the function was taken over by Chennai Metropolitan Development Authority (CMDA). The growth of Chennai did not take place in a regulated manner except in a few selected areas developed under different

Town Planning Schemes. It is also to be noticed that infrastructure facilities like water supply, sewerage communication etc. did not grow along with the rapid development of the city. The thrust given for industrial development after Independence saw the city and the metro area grown in a bigger way. The uncontrolled development was brought under control by the preparation of integrated land use plan by 1969 and the same was given to CMDA for implementation in 1973. The plan mainly dealt with land development, traffic and transportation, housing and slum clearance.

By and large the development had been taking place on the same lines as envisaged in the plan except that the satellite towns contemplated in the plan had not grown to meet the expectations. By 1995, CMDA had prepared the second master plan for CMA for the next twenty years, which liberalizes landuse controls given in earlier plans but still awaiting Government clearance. The comparison of landuse at different times in Chennai City and CMA are given in Table 3.3 and Table 3.4

**Table 3.3.**
**Landuse: Chennai City**

| Landuse | 1961 | | 1974 | | 1991 | | 2011 | |
|---|---|---|---|---|---|---|---|---|
| | Ha. | Per cent | Ha. | Per cent | Ha. | Per cent | Ha. | Per cent |
| Residential | 4290 | 33.3 | 5780 | 44.9 | 8138 | 47.7 | 7461 | 46 |
| Commercial | 420 | 3.2 | 760 | 5.9 | 1184 | 6.9 | 2202 | 13.5 |
| Industrial | 490 | 3.8 | 860 | 6.6 | 918 | 5.4 | 906 | 5.6 |
| Institutional | 3700 | 28.8 | 2160 | 16.8 | 4770 | 28.0 | 4457 | 27.5 |
| Open space | 3980 | 30.9 | 3320 | 25.8 | 2037 | 12.0 | 1203 | 7.4 |
| Total | 12880 | 100.0 | 12880 | 100.0 | 17047 | 100.0 | 16229 | 100 |

Source: Master plan for CMA, CMDA

Table 3.4.
Landuse: CMA Excluding City

| Landuse | 1964 | | 1974 | | 1991 | | 2011 | |
|---|---|---|---|---|---|---|---|---|
| | Ha. | Per cent | Ha. | Per cent | Ha. | Per cent | Ha. | Per cent |
| Residential | 3250 | 3.1 | 8460 | 8.2 | 20748 | 20.9 | 19278 | 19.4 |
| Commercial | 120 | 0.1 | 100 | 0.1 | 428 | 0.4 | 9707 | 9.8 |
| Industrial | 2460 | 2.4 | 2860 | 2.8 | 4705 | 4.7 | 7482 | 7.5 |
| Institutional | 6990 | 6.7 | 2540 | 2.4 | 5062 | 5.1 | 6544 | 6.6 |
| Open space | 4420 | 4.3 | 10720 | 10.3 | 27404 | 27.6 | 332 | 0.3 |
| Agricultural | 86550 | 83.4 | 79120 | 76.2 | 40991 | 41.3 | 55996 | 56.4 |
| Total | 103790 | 100 | 103790 | 100 | 99338 | 100 | 99338 | 100 |

Source: Master plan for CMA, CMDA

As far as residential development is concerned, the area occupied for residential use had increased in the city by 35 per cent and in the rest of CMA area by 160% during 1974. Between 1974 and 1991, the growth was phenomenal with 40.8 per cent in the city and it was 538 per cent in CMA. This reflects the rapid spread of residential development on the periphery and the diminishing area of undeveloped land left in the city for conversion to residential use.

## 3. GENERAL PROFILE OF THE CHENNAI CITY

## ADMINISTRATIVE DIVISIONS

The area of Chennai City including urban agglomeration is 174 square kilometers and the entire area has been classified as urban. The entire area comes under Chennai Corporation. There are three parliamentary constituencies and fourteen legislative assembly constituencies in Chennai City. The city is divided into 155 divisions and 10 zones and five taluks for administrative purposes. Each zone has a zonal office providing administrative and other basic amenities to the respective regions of operation.

The zone I encompasses Kodungaiyur, Tondiarpet and surrounding areas. The zone II provides administrative services to Royapuram, George Town and other areas in the near vicinity. The zone III encompasses Perambur, Pullianthope and surrounding regions. The zone IV serves the regions of Ayanavaram, Sembium etc. Annanagar, Nungambakkam are served by zone V administrative division of corporation. The zone VI consists of the Triplicane, Royapettah and surrounding areas. Egmore, Purusawalkam, Chetpet, Chintadripet etc., are included in the administrative division of zone VII. Zone VIII encloses Kodambakkam, T.Nagar and surrounding regions. Saidapet and Guindy are under zone IX and Adyar and Thiruvanmiyur falls under the zone X administrative division of Corporation.

Table 3.5 reveals the distribution of Taluks, zones, wards/divisions in Chennai city. Fort/Tondiarpet taluks and Perambur/Purusawalkam taluks has 2 zones and 31 divisions/wards each under its administration. The highest number of divisions is in Egmore/Nungambakkam(48).The lowest number of divisions is in Guindy/ Mambalam

**Table 3.5**

**Distribution of Taluks, Zones, Wards/Divisions in Chennai city**

| S.no. | Taluks | Zones | Division/Wards | Total |
|-------|--------|-------|----------------|-------|
| 1. | Fort/Tondiarpet | 2 | 1-31 | 31 |
| 2. | Perambur/Purusawalkam | 2 | 32-63 | 31 |
| 3. | Egmore/Nungambakkam | 2 | 64-78 & 97-129 | 48 |
| 4. | Mylapore/Triplicane | 2 | 76-96 & 142-155 | 33 |
| 5. | Guindy/Mambalam | 2 | 130-141 | 11 |
| | Total | | | 155 |

**Source: Statistical handbook 2001-Chennai**

## RIVERS

Two languid streams, the Cooum and the Adyar, intersect the city. Cooum runs through the heart of the city and enters the sea in-between the university buildings and the Fort. St. George underneath the Napier Bridge, while the latter wends its way through the southern part of the city and enters the sea near Adyar. These two rivers are almost stagnant and do not carry enough water except during rainy seasons. Cooum river starts from Kesavaram Anicut in Kesavaram village built across Kortaliyar river. The surplus from Cooum tank joins this course at about 8 kms. lower down and this point is actually the head of Cooum river which is located at 48 kms. west of Chennai. The river receives a sizeable quantity of sewage from its neighbourhood for disposal. Though the river Adyar can be traced to a point near Guduvancheri village, it assumes the appearance of a stream only after it receives the surplus water from the Chembarambakkam tank as wells the drainage of the areas in the southwest of Chennai. The river has no commercial importance, but the fishermen in the neighbourhood make their living by fishing in the river.

## CANALS

The Buckingham canal, which runs through the states of Tamil Nadu and Andhra Pradesh is a navigation canal. This canal runs almost parallel to the Coromandal coast within the limits of 5 kms. from the coast. It joins up a series of natural backwaters and connects all the coastal districts from Guntur to South Arcot. Entering the city at Tondiarpet in the north and running along the western outskirts of George Town, it joins the new canal, southwest of General Hospital. The other canal worth mentioning in the city is the Otteri Nullah, which commences from the village Mullam, runs eastwards upto Purasawalkam and then passes through Buckingham and Carnatic Mills and finally joins the Buckingham Canal, north of Basin Bridge Railway Station. Chennai has 25.60 kms. of sea coast which is flat and sandy for about a km. from the shore. The bed of the sea is about 42' deep and slopes further in gradual stages for a distance of about 5 kms. from the coast attaining a depth of about 63'. The two principal currents, first from the north and second from the south flow parallel to the coast. The former sets in about the middle of October and continue till February while the latter starts by about August and continues till the burst of the northeast monsoon in the middle of October. These two principal currents must be caused by the winds.

## LANGUAGES

The history of Tamilnadu dates back to Paleolithic age. The Official languages spoken in the District/State is Tamil, one of the oldest languages greatly influenced by its rich and colourful past. Concerted efforts have been made over the last decade or so to preserve the purity and identity of Tamil language. More recently there has been a steady stream of people migrating into the district from different parts of the State/country making Chennai district truly cosmopolitan in its composition. Today one can hear several languages such as Telugu, Malayalam, Gujarati, Hindi, Kannada and other

Indian languages being spoken in the Metro. Above all, the foreign tourists, industrial and other delegates need not have any fear of not being understood as English is spoken with considerable fluency in the district

## CULTURE AND LIFE STYLES

Chennai district, the capital of Tamilnadu has a legacy of ancient tradition and rich cultural heritage. Dance forms like Bharathanatyam and various forms of dance and music including Carnatic music have flourished here for centuries. The people of Chennai City lead by and large, a relaxed lifestyle. The urban social recreation includes, clubs, golf, links, beach resorts, theme parks, race courses, art and theatre. Visits to game reserves, long sandy beaches, zoological and entertainment parks are the other way of social pastimes available in the Chennai district.

## DEMOGRAPHIC BACKGROUND

The increased population growth in the city can be associated with national increase and the constant migration of the people. The population which had stabilized at around half a million at the turn of the century has now grown to more than four millions within Chennai City and to nearly six millions in the metropolitan area. The most rapid growth has taken place in the peripheral zones of the city and in the suburbs in the metropolitan area. There is, therefore, an inexorable move towards sub urbanization mainly along the road and rail transport corridors. A slowing down of the population during the Eighties and Nineties has made it possible to take stock of the problems of urban growth, and to ensure a more orderly pattern of development.

Chennai City and its surroundings had a number of water sources like tanks at Poondi, Chembarambakkam, Puzhal, Velachery, Retteri etc. and the river Adyar and Coovam and Buckimham canal. The settlement had taken place around and along the water bodies. The population growths were also on the same lines. Before the population explosion inside the city area, the per capita water availability was more.

Chennai being well connected with the rest of the world by road, rail, sea and air has attracted more people to migrate into the city in search of employment, education, medical facilities etc. The first scientific census of the city was taken in 1871 and Chennai city population then was 3.97 lakhs. As the development activities inside the city started growing, the city saw the phenomenal growth in its population size. In 1971, the population had increased to 25.72 lakhs registering a six –fold increase over a period of 100 years. The growth of population in city as well in Metropolitan area is presented in Table 3.6 and chart 3.1. The average percentage of growth of population per annum between 1931 and 1991 works out to over 3 percent both for city as well as metropolitan area.

The rate of population growth has been low, particularly since 1971 and the latest growth has only been 9.76 per cent in a period of 10 years amounting to less than one per cent per annum from 1991 to 2001. This may be due to the two possible factors – the strengthening of other cities and towns in Tamil Nadu resulting in a decline of immigration into Chennai and a decline in the birth rate caused by the social, educational and economic development. However the growth rate as estimated for Chennai city by CMDA for 2011 may not be achieved, as it is very much on the higher side. Perhaps the decadal growth rate of 26.42 percent for CMA may be achievable as it is in tune with the previous decade growth factors.

### Table 3.6
### Population growth in CMA

| Year | Chennai City | | Chennai Metropolitan Area | |
|------|------------|----------------------|------------|----------------------|
| | Population | Percentage Variation | Population | Percentage Variation |
| 1900 | | 5.41 | | 8.00 |
| 1911 | 5.56 | 2.77 | 8.30 | 3.75 |
| 1921 | 5.79 | 4.14 | 8.76 | 5.54 |
| 1931 | 7.13 | 23.14 | 10.56 | 20.55 |
| 1941 | 8.55 | 19.92 | 14.50 | 37.31 |
| 1951 | 14.16 | 65.61 | 17.62 | 21.52 |
| 1961 | 17.29 | 22.10 | 23.24 | 31.90 |
| 1971 | 24.67 | 42.68 | 34.75 | 49.53 |
| 1981 | 32.66 | 32.39 | 43.86 | 26.22 |
| 1991 | 38.41 | 17.61 | 58.46 | 33.29 |
| 2001 | 42.16 | 9.76 | 75.22 | 28.67 |
| 2011 | 60.46 | 43.41 | 95.09 | 26.42 |

**Source: Census of India 2001**

The city of Chennai, which was the fourth largest city in the country in terms of population during 1991, moved to fifth place during 2001 and now it is the second largest city in the Southern region paving way for Bangalore as per the latest census (Provisional) reports. Nevertheless the Urban Agglomeration area of Chennai accommodates more population than that of Bangalore. The first five cities in India in terms of population as per 2001 census are shown in the Table 3.7and chart 3.1

### Table 3.7
### Population of First Five Cities in India: 2001

| Name of the city | City Population | U/A Population |
|------------------|----------------|----------------|
| Greater Mumbai | 11,914,398 | 16,368,084 |
| Delhi | 9,817,439 | 12,791,458 |
| Kolkata | 4,580,544 | 13,216,546 |
| Bangalore | 4,292,223 | 5,686,844 |
| Chennai | 4,216,268 | 6,424,624 |

U/A: Urban Agglomeration
**Source: Census of India 2001**

Chart 3.1

# POPULATION GROWTH IN CMA

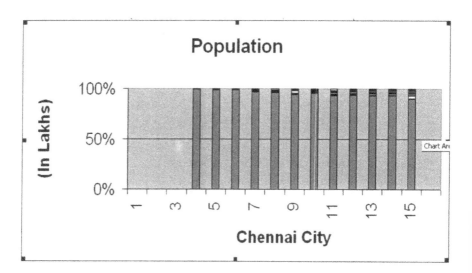

**POPULATION DENSITY**

One of the important indices of population concentration is the density of population. It is defined as the number of persons per square kilometer. The rate of growth of city area has been marginal compared to the rate of growth of population living in that area. This has resulted in a faster increase in density of population inside the city which is depicted in the Table 3.8 and shown in the chart 3.2.

Table 3.8
Density of population: Chennai

| Census year | Area (In Sq.Km) | Density (in persons Per Sq.Km) | Rate of growth in In density per year |
|---|---|---|---|
| 1871 | 71 | 5832 | - |
| 1881 | 71 | 5953 | 0.21 |
| 1891 | 71 | 6638 | 1.15 |
| 1901 | 71 | 7472 | 1.26 |
| 1911 | 71 | 7608 | 0.18 |
| 1921 | 71 | 8701 | 1.44 |
| 1931 | 75 | 9499 | 0.92 |
| 1941 | 75 | 10070 | 0.60 |
| 1951 | 129 | 10992 | 0.92 |
| 1961 | 129 | 13422 | 2.21 |
| 1971 | 129 | 19168 | 4.28 |
| 1981 | 172 | 19274 | 0.06 |
| 1991 | 172 | 22077 | 1.45 |
| 2001 | 172 | 24231 | 0.98 |

**Source: Census of India**

The Population density that was 5832 persons per square kilometer during 1871 increased about 3.5 times in 100 years and it was 19168 persons per square kilometer during 1971. Then in a span of 30 years migration into the city was much more resulting in higher density viz. 24231 persons per square kilometer. The migration into the city was highest between 1961 and 1971 with over 4 percent per annum and it was lowest

## Chart 3.2

## DENSITY OF POPULATION

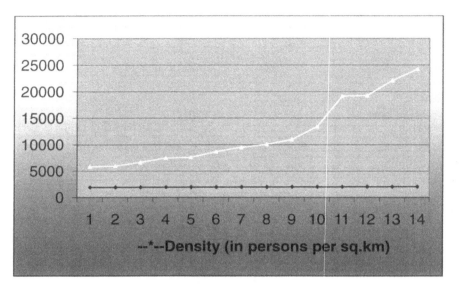

between 1961 and 1971 with over 4 percent per annum and it was lowest between 1971 and 1981 with 0.06 percent (Structure plan for Madras Metropolitan Area-Volume 1 and 2 (1985). The higher the density, the higher will be the demand for housing, water requirement, sewerage disposal and transport facilities.

## POPULATION STRUCTURE

India being the second largest country (next to China) in terms of total population has 102,70,15,247 persons as per census 2001 out of which 6,21,10,839 persons (6 percent) live in Tamil Nadu. Chennai City being the capital of Tamil Nadu accounts for around 6.78 percent of State population amounting to 42,16,268. The distribution of male and female in the total population is 21,61,605 (6.9 percent of State male population) and 20,54,663 (6.7 percent of State female population).

While India has 933 females for every males. Tamil Nadu has 986 females and Chennai has 951 females. The sex ratio per 1000 males in Chennai has increased from 934 during 1991 to 951 during 2001 as shown in the Table 3.9 and depicted in the chart 3.3

Table 3.9

Sex Ratio

|  | Total Persons | Males | Females | Sex Ratio | Density | Decadal Growth |
|---|---|---|---|---|---|---|
| India | 1,027,015,247 | 531,277,078 | 495,738,169 | 933 | 324 | 21.34 |
| Tamil Nadu | 62,110,839 | 31,268,654 | 30,842,185 | 986 | 478 | 11.19 |
| Chennai | 4,216,268 | 2,161,605 | 2,054,663 | 951 | 24231 | 9.76 |

Source: Census of India 2001

CHART 3.3

SEX RATIO

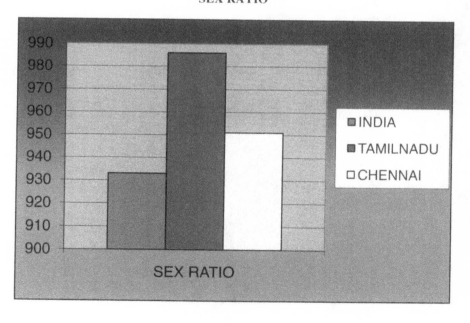

Chennai has around 3,74,089 (8.9 percent of Chennai population) children below 6 years out of which 1,90,044 (8.8 percent of male population) are male children and 1,84,045 (9.0 percent of female population) are female children (sex ratio of 968). The same trend holds good for the urban agglomeration area where there are 3,10,212 male children (9.14 percent of male population), and 2,97,451 female children (9.5 percent of female population totaling in 6,07,663 children (9.46 percent of total population). But during 1991 census, Chennai city had 4,68,508 children which means that there is decline of about 20 percent in the child population over a period of 10 years as shown in Table 3.10 and given in the chart 3.4. This may be due to adoption of one-child family norm and other social and environmental factors.

Table 3.10
Child Population

| Sex | 1991 Census | 2001 Census | Percentage of growth |
|---|---|---|---|
| Male Children | 238782 | 190044 | -20.41 |
| Female Children | 229726 | 184045 | -19.88 |
| Total Children | 468508 | 374089 | -20.15 |

Source: Census of India 2001

## Chart 3.4

## GROWTH OF CHILD POPULATION

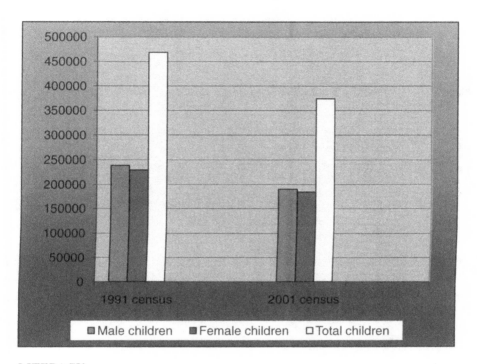

**LITERACY**

Out 4.16 lakhs population, about 30.79 lakhs are literates (Table 3.11) resulting in a reduction of literacy rate from 81.60 per cent during 1991 to 80.14 per cent during 2001. The male literacy rate has come down from 87.86 percent to 84.71 percent but there is slight increase in female literacy rate going to 75.32 percent in 2001 from 74.87 percent during 1991. Nevertheless the total literates in Chennai have increased from 27.52 lakhs to 47.69 lakhs resulting in an increase of about 73 percent as shown in Table 3.11 and in chart 3.5. Among the districts of Tamilnadu, Chennai with 80.14 percent ranks 4th in literacy, 1st, 2nd and 3rd being Kanyakumari, Thuthukudi, and Nilgiris with 88.11 percent, 81.96 percent, and 81.44

percent respectively. However Chennai district has registered higher literacy rate than the state average of 73.4 per cent.

Table 3.11

Demography

| Place | Urban/ Rural | Total Population (in Lakhs) | | | Literates (In Lakhs) | | | Percentage of Literates | |
|---|---|---|---|---|---|---|---|---|---|
| | | Male | Female | Total | Male | Female | Total | Male | Female |
| Tamil Nadu | Urban | 137.60 | 134.82 | 272.42 | 108.93 | 91.63 | 200.56 | 79.2 | 68.0 |
| | Rural | 175.09 | 173.60 | 348.69 | 119.55 | 86.13 | 205.68 | 68.3 | 49.6 |
| | Total | 312.69 | 308.42 | 621.10 | 228.48 | 177.77 | 406.24 | 73.1 | 57.6 |
| Chennai City | Urban | 21.62 | 20.55 | 42.16 | 16.70 | 14.09 | 30.79 | 77.3 | 68.6 |
| Chennai Urban Agglomeration | Urban | 32.94 | 31.30 | 64.25 | 25.90 | 21.80 | 47.70 | 78.6 | 69.6 |

**Source: Census of India 2001**

Table 3.12
Growth of Literacy Tate: Chennai

| Sex | 1991 Census | 2001 Census | Percentage of growth |
|---|---|---|---|
| Male literates | 1535351 | 2589870 | 68.68 |
| Female literates | 1216990 | 2179721 | 79.10 |
| Total literates | 2752341 | 4769591 | 73.29 |

**Source: Census of India 2001**

74

Chart 3.5

GROWTH OF LITERACY RATE : CHENNAI

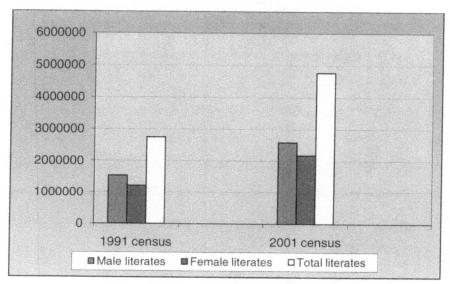

As per the latest census reports, Chennai has 14.41 lakhs workers of which about 80 per cent are males and the rest are females. Obviously, all these workers belong either to secondary or tertiary categories, and the proportion of primary workers is very much insignificant.

Table 3.13
Distribution of Workers: Chennai

| Person | Total workers | Cultivators | Agricultural Labourers | Household Industry Workers | Other workers |
|--------|---------------|-------------|------------------------|----------------------------|---------------|
| Male | 1192924 (100.00) | 425 (0.04) | 416 (0.03) | 12912 (1.08) | 1179171 (98.85) |
| Female | 248458 100.00 | 363 (0.15) | 299 (0.12) | 9196 (3.70) | 238600 (96.03) |
| Total | 1441382 (100.00) | 788 (0.06) | 715 (0.05) | 22108 (1.53) | 1417771 (98.36) |

Source: Census of India 2001
(Numbers in brackets indicate the percentage to the total)

## INFRASTRUCTURAL FACILITIES AND AMENITIES

Chennai has grown into one of the four major cities of India mainly because of availability of better communication facilities in terms of road, rail, seaport and airport and the recent development of high band width Internet connectivity.

## RAILWAYS

To cater to the commuting needs of Chennai residents, it has suburban train corridors and Mass Rapid Transit System (MRTS) in addition to intercity trains to all parts of the country. Chennai Central and Egmore railway terminals have a long-standing name in the history of Chennai. Central station has become an important railway terminal in Indian Railways. The other terminal that serves Chennai City is Egmore station with both broad and metre gauges.

## ROADS

The Corporation of Chennai maintains over 300 kilometers of roads, which are used by the city bus system. In addition to these bus-routable roads, Chennai has feeder roads, streets, and lanes to cater to road transportation. The roads within Chennai city range from 5 meters to 45 meters forming single lane to 6 lane roads. The road network is primarily based on three National Highways, leading to Calcutta (NH5), Bangalore (NH4) and Dindugul (NH45). The other roads that connect Chennai to the rest of the state include East Coast Road, Old Mahabalipuram road, Chennai-Thiruvallur Road and Chennai Ponneri road.

## INDUSTRIAL DEVELOPMENT

The pre-colonial period in Chennai had only agricultural production and household industries. Chennai saw a quick growth of industries during the post independence period, with large industries and industrial houses established in and around Chennai city. The major industrial estates were established in Ennore and Manali in the North, Avadi and Ambattur in the West and Guindy in the South of Chennai city. The early post independence period saw many production oriented industries whereas the recent industries development in the service sector. The computer software, hotels, hospitals and tourism are some of the areas of recent origin.

Even though software industry has its location spread almost throughout the city, the establishment of EL Net city, TIDEL Park Complex and IT Corridor along Old Mahabalipuram Road and the Vikram Sarabai Electronic Complex at Perungudi, Visual Graphics, Brigade Solutions, Reliance Software, SSI Info Tech and RAMCO Systems has a boon to the growth of industries in Chennai.

Chennai is known for automobile industry in India. The bus and trucks manufacturing unit (Ashok Leyland) at Ennore, automobile spare manufacturing at Ennore, Madhavaram, Padi and Ambattur, car manufacturing units at Maraimalai Nagar (50 Km from Chennai), Sriperumbudur (40 km from Chennai) and Thiruvallur have all established production centers, which require transportation by road, rail, sea and air.

Chennai finds a better place in the industrial map of India mainly because it has better infrastructure facilities in terms of road, rail, seaport and airport and communication facilities in terms of high bandwidth internet connection, stable power supply etc. In addition, the industrial developments in and around Chennai provide more direct and indirect employment opportunities, thus attracting more people into the city. The other reason for the growth of industries may be the availability of qualified and skilled personnel in Chennai.

## MEDICAL FACILITIES IN CHENNAI

Being the major city in the southern part of India, Chennai had developed into a high-end medical treatment center. It has a Government -run super specialty hospital at Park town, 5 general hospitals, 10 speciality hospitals for Gynecology, paediatrics, mental, health, thoracic medicine, dental and ophthalmic and 4 peripheral hospitals. In addition to Government hospitals, Employees State Insurance (ESI) hospitals and Chennai Municipal Corporation dispensaries are attending to the medical needs of the Chennai citizens. Railway hospital, Port Trust hospital, Police hospital and the Central Government Employees hospitals are there to cater to the needs of specified group.

Chennai has world-class private hospitals providing high quality care. Some of the important hospitals in the private sector include Apollo Hospital at Nungambakkam, Vijaya Hospital at Vadapalani, Madras Medical Mission at Mogapair, Malar Hospital at Adyar, National hospital at Royapuram, Kalliappa hospital at Raja Annamalaipuram, VHS Hospital at Adyar, MOIT Hospital at Poonamallee, Harvey Hospital at Nungambakkam, KJ Hospital at Kilpauk and the like. All the medical facilities created under Government as well as under private sector do not only cater to the residents of Chennai but also people from other part of the state and other part of the country.

## EDUCATIONAL FACILITIES

Chennai houses a number of higher learning institutes compared to other parts of the state. It acts as inducement to move to the city in search of better educational facilities. Chennai has become a center of excellence in higher education with 6 universities under its umbrella. The opening up of private participants for providing technical education has resulted in having around 36 engineering colleges, four medical colleges, 37 paramedical and dental colleges and more than 30 engineering polytechnics in addition to other regular art and science colleges.

## HOUSING IN CHENNAI CITY

Housing plays the predominant role among the primary and basic needs of the people. It plays an important role in the attitudes, health and efficiency of the labourer, which increase his productivity. Hence it is a kind of investment in the promotion of human resource development. In India housing facilities fall very short of social needs due to the scarcity of resources on one hand and the rapid growth of population on the other hand.

As done in the ancient times, people began settling down along the communication lines viz. suburban railway lines and the major corridors. Chennai City is well connected to other places of the state and to major towns and state headquarters of neighboring states by road, rail and also by air. Thus, the population that moves in or out of the city runs into a few lakhs. Chennai is recognized as one of the National Commission of Urbanization (NCU). Because of its primacy, Chennai tends to grow faster and bigger. in the context of liberalized economy. Focus on Industrial Development and entry of Multi National Companies in Industrial Sector, the pace of development of Chennai Metropolitan Area is likely to be faster. This warrants urgent measures to plan, implement and guide the developments in order to make the Metropolitan Area livable by improving its quality of life. Chennai Metropolitan Development Authority focuses its activities on various development schemes with the above concept in mind.

Chennai had early and close associations with the development of the Modern Town Planning Movement. In 1915 the eminent leader of British town planning reformist, Sir Partick Geddes (1854-1932) brought a town-planning exhibition to Madras. Geddis's futuristic vision was to clean and beautify the city with no slum living conditions. The exhibition raised consciousness planning reports and passing an enactment of Town Planning Legislation in 1920. This legislation did not provide for Geddes's futuristic vision of "city beautiful," but it established positive attitudes for including urban issues in public policy. In the real world away from the futuristic vision, India like other societies, had inequality, poverty, and the necessity to make economic life work. As we might therefore expect, slum living conditions continued in Chennai, attracting the attention of Madras Municipal Corporation in the 1940's. In consequence, in 1945 the policy makers took steps to deal with the slums, by creating the City Improvement Trust (CIT). The Trust operated within the conventional wisdom of the time, tearing down the slums and providing new housing for the residents.

Until the 1960s, housing policy in Chennai was confined to slum clearance. In 1961 the Government created the Tamil Nadu Housing Board (TNHB), reflecting the fact that the rural-urban migration and natural increase in population in Chennai were escalating the demand for housing well above the supply. The deficit in housing supply was being revealed in social statistics as a mass low-income housing problem. The private sector "permanent construction" housing catered only to the higher-income groups. The TNHB at that stage, in the 1960s, mainly saw its task as providing 'permanent construction' housing. It had two avenues through which it could add to housing supply. First, modest Government funding was provided to stimulate the Co-operative Housing Societies. These societies had grown from the success of the Co-operative principle in Tamil Nadu's agriculture. The urban necessity was for housing. Some societies provided developed plots, leaving members to make their own arrangements for building, and others provided fully developed houses. This housing was mainly allocated to the

middle and high income groups

Second, the TNHB acted as the conduit through which the Central Government housing funds could be expended in the State. These funds came through various categories and the Housing and Urban Development Corporation (HUDCO) was the Central Government's housing agent. HUDCO provided confessional interest loans for the purchase of housing build by State-Level Housing Agencies and Co-operative societies. It had limited access to capital funds, and thereby its contribution in housing supply fell short of demand. The "permanent construction" flats were beyond the financial means of low-income groups. It was the sort of approach, which the World Bank wished to change.

In 1961 the Central Government wished to see its housing programmes and its financial assistance to the States come within authorized "development" or "master plans". Accordingly it provided financial assistance for the preparation of development plans for large cities. The Tamil Nadu Government responded by commencing work on the Chennai Metropolitan Development plan in1963. It was published in 1967. The plan was in character with conventions of time. That is to say, it aimed to regulate the location and form of land use, and it reviewed the possibilities for infrastructure development over a twenty-year period, having in context the likely demographic growth. This approach is largely ineffective because it does not translate into action budgets or organizational realities, and it largely ignores change processes in the economy.

For housing, the 1961 plan merely continued its scope to the endorsement of slum clearance. But further progress was to follow in 1971 with the publication of the new Chennai Metropolitan Development Plan. The new plan shifted the emphasis from physical to economic and financial planning. In fact, the intent behind the new plan was to tap some sources of urban investment funds, which were becoming available through National and International Schemes. In housing, the 1971 Plan went far beyond the slum clearance confines of the 1967 plan.

By the mid 1970s, housing and urban policy development had an air of expectancy. The World Bank had participated in Calcutta's emergency programmes to upgrade basic utilities of the urban poor. These programmes commenced in 1972 and, along with them and without World Bank participation, the West Bengal Government began a determined and concerned effort to rid its bustees(i.e. slums) of killer and debilitating diseases. This insisted environmental Improvement Programme by getting involved in the bustees, that is, more widely into housing policy. In fact, the World Bank did join the Business Improvement programme in 1977. But the major test of the World Bank' theory of affordability, cost-recovery, replicability, would be in new development, in the form of sites and services projects. Calcutta's priorities were towards slum improvements and by cutting sites and service activities. The World Bank was ready to look for another Indian City where it all would happen. In Chennai the policy makers prepared the possibilities. In 1975 they created the Madras Metropolitan Development Authority (MMDA). The MMDA was created as a planning authority, leaving the executive development work to the TNHB and the TNSCB. But the MMDA's role could be extended to formulating the shape of low-income housing programmes and to monitoring progress made by the Executive Boards, The TNHB and TNSCB.

As we have seen, the World Bank did negotiate loan agreements in Chennai, with programme activity ready to commence in 1977. By 1980, the language and methods of affordability-cost-recovery-replicability pervaded town planning and housing administration. This was reflected in the new 1980 development plan, prepared by overseas consultants. This new plan was termed a "Structure Plan", conveying the new fashion in town planning which emphasized strategic development options rather than regulatory detail in urbanization. In housing, the Structure Plan endorsed and elaborated the World Bank's theory of affordability, cost-recover, replicability and pushed housing the policy towards volume target planning. The process of housing change, since World Bank entered into housing in Chennai in 1977, is very much about developing low-income housing policy and coming in terms with the overall volume of housing supply targets.

The profile of Chennai City discussed in this chapter covering factor like History of Chennai, Geographical and its physical features, demographic background, infrastructural details portrays that the increase in population and technological development leads to increase in housing shortages in the urban areas. Such an increasing trend leads to the development of housing sector by offering housing finance by various housing finance institutions.

# HOUSING FINANCE – AN OVERVIEW

# CHAPTER IV

## HOUSING FINANCE –AN OVERVIEW

Finance is the life blood of every activity done, it assumes a crucial role in the housing sector too and needs huge capital outlays as compared to other necessaries like education, food, clothing and so on. The housing finance business has undergone tremendous changes in recent years. Stable property prices, a declining interest rate regime, friendly procedures, quicker clearance and better tax advantages have all gone to make housing financing the fastest growing segment in personal finance.

Housing finance constitutes a very important economic activity which serves to fulfill several objectives such as provision of shelter to needy, improvement in the quality of life, creation of an environment conductive for both health and sanitation, creation of employment opportunities, achievement of urban, rural and interpersonal equity in terms of standard of living and above all in the generation of additional voluntary savings at all levels.

This chapter makes an attempt to bring out the relationship between the national level housing shortages and the various institutions offering housing finance. A brief description of National housing and habitat policy and its characteristics are given. Housing finance system, trends of urbanization and the global perspective of housing finance has also be taken for discussion. In this chapter an overview of housing finance is presented in terms of:

1. Trends of Urbanization in India
2. Housing in India
3. Housing Scenario during the plan period
4. Housing Finance – A Global perspective
5. Housing Finance System and policy in India
6. Institutions providing housing finance

## 1. TRENDS OF URBANIZATION IN INDIA

Urbanization is the economic and demographic growth process of the urban centers. Urbanization as a process reveals itself through temporal, spatial and sectorical changes in the demographic, social economic, technological and environmental aspects of life in a given society.

A demographic analysis of urbanization in India shows that though the level of urbanization in terms of the proportion of urban population which is 27.78 per cent according to 2001 census is low, the urban population in absolute terms is enormous i.e. 285.36 millions as per 2001 census which exceed the total population of the developed countries of the world.[1]

The following table clearly highlights the Urbanization trends in India from 1901 to 2001.

Table 4.1.
Indian Urbanization Trend

| Census Year | Total Population (in millions) | Urban Population (in millions) | Decennial Growth rate Of Urban Population (per cent) | Percentage of the urbans to Total Population | Annual Exponential Growth rate |
|---|---|---|---|---|---|
| 1901 | 238.10 | 25.85 | | 10.8 | |
| 1911 | 252.09 | 25.94 | 0.35 | 10.3 | 0.03 |
| 1921 | 252.32 | 28.09 | 8.27 | 11.2 | 0.79 |
| 1931 | 278.98 | 33.46 | 19.12 | 12.0 | 1.75 |
| 1941 | 318.66 | 44.15 | 31.97 | 13.9 | 2.77 |
| 1951 | 361.09 | 62.44 | 41.42 | 17.6 | 3.47 |
| 1961 | 439.24 | 78.74 | 26.41 | 18.0 | 2.34 |
| 1971 | 548.16 | 109.09 | 38.23 | 19.9 | 3.21 |
| 1981 | 685.18 | 159.73 | 46.14 | 23.3 | 3.83 |
| 1991 | 844.33 | 217.18 | 36.19 | 25.7 | 3.09 |
| 2001 | 1027.02 | 285.30 | 31.40 | 27.78 | 2.71 |

Source: Census of India 2001.

---

[1] NARASIMHULU .K, **Census 2001 & Human Development in India**, (Serial Publications, 2004), p.13.

From the above table it is clear that urbanization trends in India increased steadily upto 1951 and declined in 1961. As compared to the decade 1971-81, the decennial growth rate of 1981-91 declined by 10 points. In the decade 1991-2001, the growth of urban population is 31.40, and it again declined by 5 points than the earlier decade. The growth rate has been declined since 1981. The reason for this slowing down of growth rate is due to slowness in economic development. The overall economic development during 1981-91 did not commensurate with the changing upward trend in population growth.

Due to increasing urbanization, providing houses to all the people have become a serious problem. Rents are high in the urban areas and even middle class families live in slums. Another serious consequence of urbanization is the mushroom growth slums in cities and towns. City attracts migrates from surrounding rural and semi-urban areas, who develop slum colonies in the city. These slums are above of poverty and diseases. Urban industrialization lead to the pollution of water, air. Noise and land. There is lot of congestion and unhealthy conditions due to slums. Water pollution leads to the outbreak of epidemics and high traffic on roads in urban areas leads to lot of noise and air pollution.

The discussion so far made centered around the trends of urbanization in India. Before Studying the Housing Finance, it is a must to have an overall idea of housing trends in India.

## 2. HOUSING IN INDIA

Despite the country's achievements in different fields over the last quarter century, India has yet adequately to tackle one of its basic needs that of housing for its teaming millions. The 548 million people in the country live as 97 million families or households in 93 million housing units[2]. The housing situation in the Country is not as satisfactory or hopeful as the ratio of households to the stock of houses. In addition to an outright shortage of four million houses, which would suggest that more than one family lives in a single room or tenement, about 19 million houses fall below accepted standards of habitation.

Housing disparities in rural and urban areas by different income group patterns of ownership and the leasing accommodation and building sites have not undergone much change during the past decade. The disparities in status as between the urban and rural areas are apparent. The ownership rate is high in the low and highest size classes in the urban areas. People living in their own houses, whether in village, town or city, generally occupy more floor area or enclosed volumes of space than others who live a rented houses[3].

Moreover the housing situation in each of the Northern, Eastern, Western and Southern zones of India differ from one another in design, materials, technology, floor space available, ownership and aggregation patterns inhabiting dwelling units, etc., which largely reflect the environment and socio-economic conditions prevalent in the area. The detailed regional studies could postulate useful correlations.

---

[2] SHELTER, ENVIRONMENT AND HABITAT, - **Basic issues in Developing Countries.** (Key note address by, Bhaskara Rao to Earoph VI Congress, ITPI, silver jubilee international conference, Bangalore, February 15-25, 1978), p.43.
[3] Ibid, p.43

## Main issues in housing

Housing is as varied and complex as the society is. However, income, size of the city, rate of urban growth and policy are certain constraint features, which dominate and shape housing shortage.

Land being a factor of production, its availability is limited due to the ever increasing demand. For every 10 lakhs additional units atleast 6000 hectares of developed land is required. Land prices depend on accessibility which vary greatly among different types of cities. When there is ready access to urban cities in large cities, land is scarce and therefore high priced. Land in the outskirts of such cities are cheaper due to the fact that provision of water, sewerage and other services have failed to keep pace with urban expansion.

## Housing Demand

Housing is a commodity and in the housing market there are many buyers and sellers, but each individual on his own cannot play a dominant role in the market. There may be competition and collusion among buyers and sellers and free entry or exit is open for both. Consumers have continuous, transitive and established preferences for wide ranging alternate choice of housing and non-housing goods. If consumers try to maximize housing satisfaction from household activities, where housing is a basic component, they will have to extend the same to other activities also. There could be restrictions of place and demand depending upon the nature of housing services and the resources used to produce these services. For example, house purchases may be subject to finance, availability of quality of construction and preferred housing services. If the household had rational and complete preference, ordering by maximizing satisfaction it is possible to express the demand for housing as a function of household income, the price of housing, the price of all other commodities and the nature of requirements in the specific region.

The estimation of housing demand is beset by many problems. Since sub-markets may exist in the housing market, identification of the same becomes crucial. In many sub-markets, housing supply arises from the rental and turnover cost seconded by housing cost. Housing supply and demand in most sub-markets may be simultaneously determined. Where housing is a complete commodity, multiple attributes are traded in the market for which individual prices are not observed. Housing is a complex, multi-dimensional commodity. As durable asset, housing structure provides both consumption and investment services and may be purchased with a loan or other forms of assistance. The housing stock, which is standing, is characterized by situational attributes defined in social or in economic terms. There may exist frictional and search costs, which are significant enough to influence the demand.

The durability of housing unit is a major characteristic of the standing stock. This specifies the nature of satisfaction from housing and the income constraint. Since housing is a basic need, decision on housing expenditure has to take a long-term projection. If the household wants to be consistent, only normal income is to be considered which is derived through an average of past and future earnings. It may be that the housing loan over years may ration out the normal and other household expenditure. Where housing assets appreciate more rapidly than many other assets and when appreciation rates are higher than the mortgage rate, permanent income will partly depend upon housing expenditure pattern.[4]

**Housing supply**

Housing supply includes supplies of existing stock facing different supply technologies or factor prices and also supplies conversion. Housing construction is an important macro economic magnitude and constitutes about one third of all construction sector output. The construction sector is extremely susceptible to the policy action of Central and State Government.

Availability of credit to contractors, who want to construct houses for individuals, and to promoters, availability of long term loans at a reasonable rate of interest, availability of building materials and favourable tax laws related to property are some of the factors determining the supply of housing. Availability of loans at a reasonable rate of interest to entrepreneurs for a longer period of time is one of the factors influencing the supply of housing. This is so because the cost of investment in housing will become less. This factor may influence the decision of the people to buy houses and thereby the supply housing.

The supply of housing also to a certain extent depends upon the availability of building material such as steel, cement etc, which in turn depends upon the development of infrastructure facilities. Uninterrupted supply of building material helps in the reduction of construction cost and thereby the supply of houses. This is also emphasized by the Redcliffs Committee as "The Credit availability to be crucial

---

[4]GIRIAPPA S., **Housing Finance and Development in India**, (Mohit Publications, New Delhi, 1998), p.2

for financing construction, addition to stocks and other regular item of expenditure"[5]. Liberal tax and property laws of the country will also influence the supply of housing by encouraging people to make investment in housing. Accumulated backlog of housing needs comprises the number of dwelling units required to accommodate that part of the population which can be said to have been living in overcrowded, unsanitary or unimproved housing, which us practically homeless.

Having studied the factors influencing the demand and supply of housing sector, an attempt is made here to study the economic values of housing.

From the long term point of view of its economic value, any investment in housing at present, due to the prevailing inflationary conditions among others will be appreciated. In turn, the economic development of a country also depends upon the total investment made by the people on housing activities as also the structure, and design of houses and the standard of living of the people.

It may be argued that housing is a tool of economic development because an investment in housing increases employment opportunities, income of the people and the savings of the country. The higher rate of savings in turn helps further investment and creates a multiplier effect in all the different sectors of the economy, ultimately leading to the economic development of a country.

Thus investment in housing acts as a tool of economic development. Housing is a labour intensive industry and it facilitates redistribution of income. A reasonable portion of the investment made in housing sector goes to the labour directly by way

[5] REPORT OF THE COMMITTEE ON WORKING ON MONITORY SYSTEM, **London, HMSO,** (1959) p.132

of wages. This generates additional income in the hands of the poor people who occupy the lower strata of life.

In the modern society, man spends up to 70 per cent of his life span in his house. Comfortable housing plays a vital role in developing and improving the physical, mental and cultural conditions of the human being, thereby accelerating his efficiency. This in turn becomes a strong motivator of human capital formation.

## HOUSING MARKET

In the housing market, individual transacts infrequently while a non-moving household may acquire broad continuous stream of market information. The specific information enquired for purchase will only accrue with purposive search. The quality of information stored in the individual's memory is likely to decay over time. This loss is compounded by changes in the housing market in the non-moving period. However, imperfect information and the possibility of making false bids do not result in search across the sub-markets. Since housing is a major act of consumption and investment, a sub-optimal purchase may result in a serious loss of satisfaction. In the evaluation of purchase in housing market various institutions may shape household types and choices. Special segregation of purchasing opportunities adds to the time, travel, and psychic cost of housing search. The house purchase process requires individuals not only to evaluate dispersed housing offers and to pursue housing finance, but also to have an access for placement of bids. This may generate friction but it may remain relatively constant over time if the housing market evolves in a stable fashion. Sub-market demands may change more rapidly than the supply because of slow rate of turnover of second hand housing stock.[6]

## HOUSING LOAN MARKET IN INDIA

The size of mortgage loan market in India is relatively very small compared to developed countries. Our estimated size of mortgage loans with HFCs is about Rs.32,000 crores. In developed countries like UK and USA, the outstanding mortgage loan to GDP is above 55 per cent, Japan 33 per cent, Korea over 10 percent, in Malaysia over 20 per cent and Hongkong over 30 per cent. In India the ratio is just around 1.6 per cent. After including other indirect agencies like Government and financing Institutions, the percentage share will be less than 2 per cent. However, new mortgage loans as percentage of GDP is 11 per cent in USA and 9 per cent in U.K. i.e. about 20 per cent of outstanding, whereas in India it is 0.6 per cent. i.e. about 37 per cent of outstanding.[7]

The mortgage loans are long term loans for 15 to 20 years. In some countries such as Japan these are also available for 25 to 30 years. There are very limited options for availability of funds for such a long period and at a fixed interest rate. The long term Debt market has not so far developed or stabilized in India. Most of the institutions are suffering from asset liability mismatch and the consequences would be felt when liabilities will mature for payment. The interest rate risk will be exposed once the interest rates start moving northwards.[8]

---

[6] GIRIAPPA S, **op.cit.**, p.9
[7] INDUSTRIAL ECONOMIST, **Economic awareness series,** (National seminar on housing, ushering in the grey revolution, policy issues, Chennai, November, 17, 2001), p.2.
[8] INDUSTRIAL ECONOMIST, **op.cit.**, p.3

## HOUSING SHORTAGE IN INDIA

Housing was one of the sectors that the Government wanted to focus on in view of the acute shortage of the acute shortage of dwelling units in the country.[9] Gaining an idea about the present situation relating housing is a precondition to plan for the future development of housing. Most of the people in India are homeless. They live only in rental houses without adequate amenities like water, toilets, etc. Increase in population has contributed to the heavy demand for houses in India, which in turn has resulted in the increased demand for financial assistance from the organised finance institutions. The Shortage of houses and the increase in population are given below for a clear understanding of the position in India.

Table 4.2
Housing Shortage in India (in million)

| Census Year | Housing Shortage | | Total |
|---|---|---|---|
| | Rural | Urban | |
| 1951 | 5.8 | 3.1 | 8.9 |
| 1961 | 6.6 | 3.6 | 10.2 |
| 1971 | 11.6 | 2.9 | 14.5 |
| 1981 | 16.10 | 5.0 | 21.10 |
| 1991 | 20.6 | 10.4 | 31.00 |
| 2001 | 26.5 | 19.4 | 45.9 |

Source: Handbook of Housing Statistics 2001

It could be seen from the Table 4.2 that the shortage of houses has increased from 8.9 million in 1951 to 45.9 million in 2001. Even the analysis with regard to housing shortage of urban and rural areas also reflects that the shortage of houses has

[9]MR. EDWARD FALERIO, **Bank Loans for house building may be made obligatory**, (The Hindu, Friday, December 30, 1988).

increased to more than 400 per cent. Increase in the shortage of housing between urban and rural areas is comparatively higher than that in the urban areas. From the above analysis it is clear that because of the increase in the population in our country, the shortage of houses has also gone up. For meeting the acute challenge situation in the country, there is a vital need for evolving an efficient planning technique for designing and execution of schemes with utmost achievement of economy and speedy action-oriented programme of quick decisive policies.[10]

## HOUSING POSITION IN INDIA

India's population has already crossed a mark of 1 billion and it is estimated that by the year 2021, 350 million people will be added with further concentration of population in urban center up to 12 percent. According to Census of 2001, India had total residential housing stock of 187 million with only 51 percent permanent dwelling units. Furthermore, out of this housing stock 54 per cent have no sanitation facility, nearly 85 per cent do not have electricity and more than 22 per cent do not have drainage facility. The lack of basic infrastructure facilities in present housing stock and the shortfall indicates chronic shortage of dwelling units with basic needs. Moreover, it is estimated that by the year 2021 the population of urban poor will be nearly 180 million.

This indicates that with present pace of growth, urban centers will face chaotic conditions for housing provision and the shanty image of our cities will create a question over environmental sustainability of human settlements. To ameliorate housing conditions in deteriorating slums radical changes are required in present land

---

[10] JAIN A.K. & GOPAL BHARGAVA, **Evolving an Urban Housing Policy,** (Abhinav publications, New Delhi), p.164

policies assuring tenure security. However, by and large government strategies on slum relocation or redevelopment have failed. Furthermore, it was recognised that private sector housing market excludes a large segment of population under poverty line in the urban centers due to limited profitability. This implies that there is a need for a reorientation in the present notions of housing provision by public intervention, which becomes an urgent need to provide housing for all.

According to an estimate India had a chronic shortage of 21.23 million dwelling units, out of which 36 per cent are required in urban centers. The Ninth Five-Year plan suggests that there is a need to build / upgrade 10 million dwelling units for urban poor or EWS and 5 million for LIG in the urban centers alone. Considering the present rate of supply of urban housing, the future rate of supply has to be accelerated three times to eradicate housing problem in urban areas. However, it seems to be difficult for public sector agencies to accelerate rate of housing provision looking at limited financial resources of Rs. 34,000 crore in comparison to required investment of Rs. 1,21,370 crore for urban centers.

The present crisis in the housing sector and dilapidated living condition of LIG and EWS segments is largely due to inappropriate government interventions. Although, government has used various strategies to fulfill housing demand, the current state of affair indicates alarming level of backlog in affordable housing especially to LIG and EWS segments. This along with ever increasing shortfall leads to exponential growth in housing demand.

In such scenario, government relied upon private real estate developers to fill the gap in housing demand; however, the recession in the last decade affected it largely. After seven years of downside since 1993, housing market in India has witnessed upswing registering five to eight percent increase in the first quarter of this year. However, according to Colliers international, the rise has been primarily in newly constructed properties due to activation of actual users. A property investment review by Knight Frank reports that the residential market has been activated due to low interest rates and competition among housing finance companies and budgetary soaps. When interest rates have fallen dramatically over the last three years, there is a possibility that borrowers would prepay their loans to take advantage of lower margins on fresh loan. According to Business Line (2003) customers would gain more by prepaying housing loans rather than investing any surplus as interest rate for loan disbursed by HDFC from 1993 to 2000 was much higher than what prevails now. This syndrome suspects probability of a higher level of repayment in the range of 12-14 percent. As a result the housing finance industry has witnessed high portfolio growth rates of 36 percent and 40 percent in last two years respectively as reported by the Credit Rating and Information Services of India Ltd (CRISIL). Furthermore, the amendments in the Finance Bill 2001 allow deduction of an amount equivalent to the total interest paid on housing loan from the taxable income up to a limit of Rs.1,50,000 in case of self occupied properties and for rental properties there is no ceiling. In addition rebate is also given on principal repayment under section 88 of the Income Tax Act.[11] This suggests that to take advantage of government incentives under the section 88 and section 24 of the Income Tax Act, prospective buyers will consider option of housing loan rather than self-financing. The lower

---

[11] NAGARAJAN. V. **A Guide to Home Loans**, (Volume 1, Issue 1, 2002 Chennai), p.41

interest rate offers substitution of rentals with EMI with a possibility of increased purchasing power of buyers and has lead to active real estate market. The Knight Frank survey of property trends in Mumbai, Delhi, Banglore, and Pune reveals that after recent stabilisation in real estate market, individuals and institutions look forwards to invest in order to yield returns between 12-18 percent. For example, HDFC has invested around Rs. 1,000 crore in commercial real estate in Banglore, Pune and Hyderabad totaling 329,000 sq.ft, while ICICI has bought 300,000 sq.ft in Banglore and Hyderabad to lease it out. Confirming the trend a report of Knight Frank estimates that 90% of all commercial property transactions in the last five years have been leasehold. The average yield from commercial property's leave-and-license agreement with a lengthy lock-in period can yield as high as 17-23 per cent returns outstripping the return from equity or gilds. A strategy integral to a decision whether to own or lease involve minimum capital investment, maximum flexibility and easier exit possibility in response to volatile real estate market.

## HOUSING –ENGINE OF ECONOMIC GROWTH

Unlike certain industries where there has been some sort of stagnation in the recent past, the scenario is different in the case of housing industry. The housing sector in the country which was passing through a recessionary phase has witnessed dramatic changes over the last few years coupled with the much needed recovery from the recessionary trends and gaining a never-before buoyancy. In a lackluster economic scenario, housing is among a few sectors to have defied the adverse trend. The last couple of years saw the fast transformation of housing sector into a crucial sector of the economy. The reversal of the recession in real estate and housing sector set in motion a few years back has been gaining further acceleration.

A host of factors have contributed to the buoyancy in the housing sector. In its continued thrust on housing, the Union Budgets during the past few years have taken several measures to extend fiscal incentives and simplify procedures that have gone a long way in giving a significant impetus to the housing sector. Apart from the Government support, factors such as increasing number of dual income families, high salaried employees with high purchasing and borrowing powers, bottoming out of property prices, decreasing interest rates, easy availability of home finance, a stock market shy of regaining its earlier momentum etc. have contributed in a significant measure to the resurgence of the housing sector. The Government of India have also been adopting several measures to encourage NRI investment in housing and real estate development for promoting the flow of foreign exchange to the country.

Housing has always been an important agenda for the Government of India over the years because it is a visible output where the development can be seen and a vital sector of the national economy creating jobs and generating taxes and wages that positively influence the quality of life. The Working Group on Urban Housing for the 9th Plan gave a thrust to housing development and targeted construction of 8.87 million housing units. The National Housing and Habitat Policy 1998 emphasises "Housing for all" by the end of 2007 together with services, social infrastructure, strong public-private partnerships and the role of the co-operative and corporate sectors.

Housing is a basic necessity as well as, being a vital part of the construction sector, an important factor of the economy. Construction activity accounts for more than 50 per cent of the development outlays and a study instituted by HUDCO to evaluate the impact of investment in the housing sector on GDP and employment has found that housing sector ranks third among the fourteen major sectors in terms of total linkage effect with other sectors of the national economy. In terms of income multiplier, it ranks fourth and is ahead of other sectors like transport and agriculture. It is estimated that a unit increase in the final expenditure would generate additional income as high as five times. As such, housing acts as a major contributor of employment and income generation and helps the individuals both directly and indirectly in their socio-economic development. Thus the government policies on the housing front have a direct impact on the health of the economy.

The Government of India has been transforming housing sector into an engine of economic growth through prudent policies and a host of initiatives including the extension of benefits u/s 80 I to mass housing projects, scrapping of Urban Land Ceiling Act, increased rebates for housing loans, increased depreciation for employee housing, lower interest rates, securitisation of housing loan etc. The recognition accorded by the Government to the real estate sector, especially the housing sector, has been quite encouraging. Even the McKinsey report presented to the Honourable Prime Minister has emphasized that housing must be accorded highest priority to accelerate GDP growth. World Bank has recognized that policies to promote free markets lead to healthy sectors which in turn help drive economic growth, a phenomenon which we are now witnessing in India. Many underdeveloped as well as developing countries have used housing reforms as an instrument to improve the GDP. There is an increasing realization globally that housing is a productive sector of the economy rather than a form of welfare. Research has clearly demonstrated that in most countries housing has the potential of becoming an engine of economic growth because of its high yield on invested resources, a high multiplier effect and a host of beneficial forward and backward linkages in the economy. It is a fact that increased housing activities give impetus to the economy with enhanced capacity utilization of related industries such as steel, cement, transportation etc. leading to an increase in revenue by way of excise and other taxes. The per capita consumption of cement has gone up from 57 kg in 1990 to 97 kg in 2000. Similarly, revival of the housing sector has had a significant impact on the steel industry, paint industry etc. More of property acquisition under increased housing activity results in more revenue to the government by way of stamp duty. Apart from a rise in the business of dealers of building materials, jobs and professions of builders and developers, architects, civil engineers, property valuers, contractors, plumbers, interior decorators, furnishers etc. thrive when housing activities take an upswing, a phenomenon which we are actually witnessing now. The economic impact of housing does not end when a home is sold and the new owner moves in. In fact, housing continues to be an economic force long after the sale is closed through activities such as furnishing, decorating, remodeling rooms, repairs, extensions, property alterations etc.

Another important aspect is that the demand for institutional finance for housing has been on a steady increase over the years resulting in the entry of a large number of players into the housing finance scene. According to the National Housing

Bank statistics, loan disbursements by commercial banks and housing finance companies to the housing sector went up to Rs.25400 crore in 2001-2002 from about Rs.22000 crore in the previous year and is likely to grow by 30 per cent this year. Fuelled by the demand for home credit, especially due to falling interest rates, the housing finance sector's incremental fund requirement is pegged at Rs.140000 crore over the next five years according to a sectoral study by Cris-Infac. The incremental direct disbursements for the housing sector is likely to grow by 24.1 per cent over the next five years, according to the study. The housing finance sector which is thus poised to register an impressive growth in the years ahead has emerged as a crucial sector in the country's economy.

The Indian economy has posted 6 per cent growth in the first quarter of 2002-2003 as against 3.5 per cent growth recorded in the first quarter of 2001-2002. It is pertinent to note that while industrial sector has shown 3.8 per cent growth as against 2.7 per cent and agricultural sector showed 4.4 per cent growth as against 1.1 per cent, construction sector has shown 6.3 per cent growth as against negative 0.2 per cent. The boost being received by the construction sector is evident from this. The resurgence in the construction sector also indicates an overall-revival of the country's economy on account of its linkages with many sectors of the economy.

Traditionally in India, most people used to depend on their provident fund and gratuity amounts received after retirement – while considering buying a home. However, with the emergence of housing finance as a major business in the country, an increasingly large number of people are going in for home loans. Socially too, India has changed, and there is no stigma attached today to going in for borrowed funds. Incomes of families are rising and their purchasing capacity as well as loan repaying capacities are going up. Property prices are more or less on a stabilizing trend. A large number of home loan options are available. HFCs are becoming increasingly liberal. Interest rates have been progressively falling. The Government of India has been giving substantial encouragements to the housing sector. The social structure of the Indian families is going through a sea change as the joint family is fast giving way to the nuclear family concept.

The pressure to have one's own home is high among these families. It is believed that the satellite towns that are being developed in many parts of the country will drive the demand for housing finance because they will cater more to the common man's housing needs. The phenomena being witnessed in the stock market are leading people to believe that the time tested avenues of investment like real estate with significant appreciation over the years are a safer bet and a safer hedge against inflation. The Government of India had recently made the development of the housing sector a priority both from the demand and the supply side by fiscal concessions to the providers of the house and to the borrowers.

With the increasing migration of people to the urban centers, shortage of housing will continue to increase and perhaps with the rapid growth of population, this is unstoppable. The National Housing Policy document estimates a housing shortage of 23 million units and the need to invest over Rs.4,00,000 crores over 10 years. Thus there will be a massive flow of funds to the housing sector in the days ahead and with the ever increasing encouragement from the Government of India, the housing sector of the country remains poised for a spectacular growth acting as a catalyst in the growth of the economy, a powerful engine of economic development.

## HOUSING IN TAMILNADU

Shelter is the basic human requirement that needs to be met on priority basis. Investments improves both working and living environment. The housing stock coupled with education, health and water supply adds to the productivity of labour force.

The demand for housing increases due to growth of population, rapid pace of industrialisation and urbanisation. As per the National Family Health Survey (1998-99), about one-third of the houses in Tamil Nadu were kutcha, while semi-pucca houses accounted for 38.4 percent and the pucca houses 27.6 percent. The proportion of kutchahouses is relatively higher in rural areas as compared to 16.7 percent in urban areas. 72 percent of the urban houses have toilet facilities. In the context of increasing pressure of population, renewal of existing houses and building up of new dwelling houses are a pre-requisite. The National Housing and Habitat Policy 1998 has specifically advocated that Government create a facilitating environment for growth of housing activity instead of taking on the task of housing itself.

The State is providing a catalytic role in providing housing stock. The Tamil Nadu Housing Board, Co-operative Housing, Tamil Nadu Slum Clearance Board are playing a major role in the creation of housing facilities in Tamil Nadu. The major sources for funding housing activity in the State are Housing and Urban Development Corporation limited (HUDCO), the State Government, LIC, HDFC and Commercial Banks. The housing stock has been steadily increasing in the State over the year with the financial help from these agencies. According to house listing operations in Censes 2001, the position was as follows:

Table 4.3
Household Position in India and Tamilnadu

| HOUSEHOLDS | TAMILNADU | INDIA |
|---|---|---|
| Total Number of households | 14,173,626 | 191,963,935 |
| Per cent of Households living in Permanent Census Houses | 58.52 | 51.80 |
| Per cent of Households living in Temporary Census Houses | 23.31 | 18.14 |

SOURCE: Tenth five year plan (2002-2007)

The policy of the Government of Tamil Nadu is to ensure the basic need, shelter for all. In order to achieve the ambitious goal of providing *"A house for each family"*, various schemes are being implemented.[12] The demand for housing is on the increase day by day due to population growth and also migration towards urban centres in search of better employment Added to this, in the changing circumstances, there has been an increased demand and desire to own houses. So the policy includes facilitating the provision of adequate houses, house sites, and cost effective/ environment friendly technologies for all categories of people. Tamil Nadu stands 2nd in the rank of ratio of urban population in 2001 next to Maharastra among the bigger states as against 5th rank in 1991 Tamil Nadu has registered an urban population growth rate of 42.79 per cent in the last decade. Considering the growth of

---

[12] TENTH FIVE YEAR PLAN (2002-2007) – **objectives, strategies, Goals & outlay**, Government of India

population every year, Tamil Nadu needs an additional 2.50 lakh houses to bridge the gap.

## Tenth Plan Outlay for Housing Sector and Estimation of Housing Stock in Tamil Nadu:

A sum of Rs.4403 crores had been earmarked of housing sector. The plan envisaged a creating of 6.85 lakh housing units for the entire State. Out of six agencies involved in creation of housing stock in the State, the Tamil Nadu Co-operative Housing Federation is a single largest category accounting for 48 per cent of the total housing stock proposed to be created, followed by Rural Development Department 22.48 per cent during the Tenth Plan period. With respect to urban areas, it is estimated that the housing stock has to increase at the rate of 0.50 lakhs[13] annually, given the current rise in the growth of urban population.

Having studied housing demand, supply, loan market, present housing position in India and Tamil Nadu, an attempt has been made to study the role played by the Government of India in housing sector through five year plans

## 3. HOUSING SCENARIO DURING THE PLAN PERIOD

The housing scenario in India has, in recent years, seen significant changes in terms of roles and functioning of the concerned agencies in the public and private sectors and their production practices. It may, however, be difficult to attribute all these changes to the impact of the GSS on the policies and programmes in India. The genesis of these changes goes back to the early 1980's when certain important

[13] ECONOMIC APPRAISAL TAMIL NADU, 2003-04 & 2004-05, **Evaluation and applied research Department,** Government of Tamil Nadu, p.157

measures were adopted to curb the subsidies in the housing sector and make the agencies financially accountable, if not self-sufficient.

An assessment of the changes in the inter-sectoral distribution of plan funds requires an analysis of the long-term trend. Consequently, the allocation pattern during the entire post-Independence period had been covered in this sub-section. It may be observed that housing activities had been at a low key during the post-Independence period. Only meager investments were made in housing during the colonial period, resulting in a serious housing shortage in many of the big cities. After Independence in 1947, partition aggravated the problem as it dislocated people and brought a large number of them into a few metropolitan cities, particularly Calcutta and Delhi. To meet the crisis, a major rehabilitation programme was launched along with various housing schemes in the First Five Year Plan(1950-1955).

As per reliable statistics the number of houses in urban areas are not available. On account of war and post war difficulties the population as per 1941-51 census the rural population increased by 7.4 per cent and urban population by 53.77 per cent. The shortage in urban areas was 18.4 lakhs during this period. The housing policy as per this plan are:

➢ Industrial housing schemes was introduced in the year 1949. As per this scheme interest free loans were provided by the central government to the state governments or private employers provided the housing cost should not exceed two-thirds of the housing scheme. The houses constructed would remain the property of the employers.

- Housing subsidies was announced by the central government. It recommended a subsidy of 50 per cent to the state governments for total construction, which includes the land costs too. The subsidy is also admissible to private employers of labour and co-operative societies of industrial workers was limited to 25 per cent of the total cost construction which includes land costs. Current rates of interests was recommended. The loans should be repayable within 25 years. In case of loans provided to co-operative societies of industrial workers and private employers should be repaid within 15 years and loans are admissible upto 37 ½ per cent of actual construction including land cost.

- Loans was also made available to LIG and MIG groups through co-operative building societies at a reasonable rate of interest.

- The Central assistance towards industrial housing finance in the five year period was Rs.13.5 crores and a contribution of Rs.15 crores from the employers and workers. The contribution by state governments was Rs.3.7 crores. Another way of raising finance was through providend fund. Under this scheme Rs.15 to Rs.16 crores was expected as collection.

- A provision of Rs.38.5 crores was made.

- Private sector investment worth Rs.900 crores in housing sector.[14]

In the Second Five year Plan (1956-1960), housing constituted 2.5 per cent of the outlay (the actual expenditure however was much less), which was higher than the

---

[14] FIRST FIVE YEAR PLAN DOCUMENT, **Government of India**, New Delhi.

corresponding figure of 2.1 percent in the First Plan, although the expenditure on rehabilitation was brought down from about 6 per cent to just 1 per cent. The housing programmes undertaken during the second five year plan, the targets adopted are:

Table 4.4
Number of houses planned for the Second Five Year Plan

| S.NO. | TYPE OF HOUSING | NO. OF HOUSES |
|-------|-----------------|---------------|
| 1. | Subsidised industrial housing | 1,28,000 |
| 2. | LIG | 68,000 |
| 3. | Rehousing of slum dwellers including sweepers | 1,10,000 |
| 4. | MIG | 5,000 |
| 5. | Plantation Labour housing | 11,000 |
| | TOTAL | 3,22,000 |

Source: Second Five year Plan

The Second five year plan was a benefit for scheduled castes, scheduled tribes, backward classes and weavers etc. During this plan the LIC of India started to provide funds for house building to middle income groups and state governments.

The Third Five Year Plan (1960-1965) allocated 2.72 percent of the public-sector outlay to housing and urban development, including water supply and sanitation, which was much less than the corresponding figures in the previous plans. The allocation for housing worked out to roughly 1.8 per cent only.[15] The planners did note the problem of inadequate funds, but suggested that "in view of the limited resources, towns and cities with population of one lakh (100,000) or more should receive priority".

The three Annual Plans that followed during 1966-1969 saw a further decline in expenditure in this combined sector, the figure coming down to 2.42 per cent. In

---

[15] III FIVE YEAR PLAN DOCUMENTS, **published by Government of India**, New Delhi.

the Fourth Five Year Plan (1969-1974), the outlay for housing, as a proportion of the total, remained at the same low level if the figure is computed after excluding the funds allocated to the Housing and Urban Development Corporation (HUDCO), and a few large (basically urban development) projects. The allocation in the Fifth Five Year Plan too was very low, (1.5 per cent) although it had set poverty eradication as an important objective. The Sixth Plan (1980-1985) allocation for housing in the relation to total public-sector outlay was reduced further but the expenditure on water supply and sanitation increased because India adopted the United Nations International Decade for Water Supply and Sanitation.

The Seventh Five Year Plan (1985-1990) stipulated that the responsibility of houses construction would gradually shift from the public to the private sector. It restricted social housing activities to the Minimum Needs Programme (MNP), for artisans and landless labourers only. The Plan allocation for housing was barely 1.3 percent. However, a special central sector scheme, called Indira Awas Yojna (IAY) for the scheduled caste/tribe population,[16] claimed over 15 per cent of the total allocation (Planning Commission, 1985). The Eighth Plan (1992-1997) approved 1.47 percent of the outlay for housing. The Eighth Plan outlay for urban housing was Rs.3,581.67 crore in the State sector and Rs.1,341.35 crore[17] in the Central Sector. Here again, targeting of the funds was to be achieved by resorting to the MNP and reserving about 20 per cent of it for IAY (Planning Commission,1992).

Capital formation in the housing sector was about 30 per cent of the total during the 1950s, which came down to 13 per cent in the 1970s at current prices. The

[16] VII FIVE YEAR PLAN DOCUMENTS published by **Government of India**, New Delhi.
[17] NABHI'S COMPILATION of **Ninth Five year plan**, 1997-2002, (A Nabhi Publication), p.599.

figure was at its lowest in 1975-1976 (10 per cent), but it stabilized subsequently at 13 per cent. Investment in housing, covering both the public and the private sectors, was as high as 34 per cent in the First Five Year Plan, which declined gradually to less than 10 per cent in the Seventh and Eighth (proposed) plans. Income from housing as a percentage of Gross Domestic Products (GDP) also declined from 3.7 in the early 1970s to 3.0 in the 1980s. Furthermore, the share of public agencies in housing investment (to total investment in this sector) has gone down over 28 per cent to less than 10 per cent over the past 40 years.

The Ninth Five Year Plan (1997-2002) has envisaged an outlay of Rs.1,50,000 crores for the housing sector as against Rs.97,500 crores during the Eighth Five Year Plan period 1992-97. Of this, Rs.38,000 crores is expected to be the net contribution of the formal sector institutions. The expected share of Housing Finance Companies (HFCs), including Housing & Urban Development Corporation Ltd.(HUDCO) was Rs.12,000 crores whereas the actual disbursement furing the very first year (1997-98) of the Ninth Five Year Plan, had been Rs.5,767.55 crores, representing a growth of 24.63 per cent as compared to the disbursement of Rs.4,627.74 crores during 1996-97. The Industrial Survey, Report, Report, 2001 conducted by 'The Hindu' emphasis that the working group on the Ninth Plan had identified the need for the provision of shelter for 16.76 million units in urban areas and 16.25 million units in rural areas for various income groups in the period 1997-2002.[18] The housing finance allocation for Commercial Banks, other than Regional Rural Banks (RRB) increased by 20.88 percent, from Rs.1071.45 crores during 1996-97 to Rs.1,295.19 crores during

---

[18] THE HINDU, **Survey of Indian Industry 2001**, (Printed and published at the National Press, Kasturi Buildings 859-860, Anna Salai, Chennai – 600 002), p.141.

1997-98. Disbursals during 1997-98 by the public sector scheduled commercial banks alone at Rs.1,454.77 crores had exceeded their level. This, along with the additionalities provided by the cooperative sector institutions and other financial institutions had substantially added to the capacity of the housing finance sector. With the result, a better integration of the housing finance system with the macro financial sector is expected to emerge in the longer run[19].

## GROSS CAPITAL OUTLAY IN HOUSING

Housing activity is a major indicator of the growth path of a nation and the quality of life it bestows on its citizens. It is however true that though our country's GDP growth rate in the last decade ranks very high, the same cannot be said about its housing sector. This activity can broadly classified as the Governmental sector and the private sector. Mass scale housing began at Governmental level as a result of arrival of displace persons pursuant to partition of the country. Initially it was undertaken as social obligation on the part of the State Government to re-house the displace persons through establishment of State Housing Boards. At the Central level it started under the banner of Delhi Development Authority(DDA) and Central Public Works Department(C.P.W.D.). Later on with emphasis on industrialization resulting in greater urbanization, all Housing Boards or specified agencies undertook various schemes such as Low Income Housing Group(LIG), Middle Income Housing Group (MIG), High Income Housing Group (HIG) and Industrial Workers Housing Schemes etc. With the beginning of planned development from 1951 onwards, the total plan outlay on housing up to the end of the Ninth Five year Plan is shown in the Table

[19] REPORT ON TREND AND PROGRESS OF HOUSING IN INDIA, **Report published by National Housing Bank,** (Mumbai, June 1988), p.53.

given below. The importance of housing sector in India can be judged by the estimate that for every rupee invested in construction of houses, 78 paise are added to GDP of the country and real estate sector is subservient to development of a number of other industries, which have backward linkages.

Table 4.5
Gross Capital Outlay on Housing in Five Year Plans, 1951-2002
(Rs. in Crores)

| PLAN PERIOD OF TOTAL | | INVESTMENT IN HOUSING | | | PERCENTAGE OF INVESTMENT |
| | | PUBLIC | PRIVATE | TOTAL | |
|---|---|---|---|---|---|
| Plan I | 1951-1956 | 250 | 900 | 1150 | 34.00 |
| Plan II | 1956-1961 | 300 | 1000 | 1300 | 19.00 |
| Plan III | 1961-1966 | 425 | 1125 | 1550 | 15.00 |
| Plan IV | 1969-1974 | 625 | 2175 | 2800 | 12.00 |
| Plan V | 1974-1979 | 796 | 3640 | 4436 | 9.30 |
| Plan VI | 1980-1985 | 1491 | 18000 | 19491 | 12.50 |
| Plan VII | 1985-1990 | 2458 | 29000 | 31458 | 9.00 |
| Plan VIII | 1992-1997 | 6377 | 18623 | 25000 | 5.75 |
| Plan IX | 1997-2002 | 7590 | 14000 | 21590 | 5.80 |

SOURCE: **Ministry of Urban Affairs, Housing Section 1997, Ninth Five-Year Plan, Indian Construction Statistics**

## CHART 4.1

### Gross Capital Outlay on housing Five Year Plan Periods
### (1951-2002)

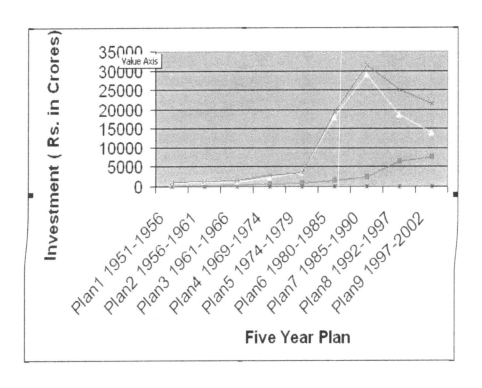

From the above table and chart it is observed that in successive Five-Year Plans the percentage of investment in housing has fallen from 34 per cent in the first Plan to 6 per cent in the Ninth Plan. Simultaneously around 1952, housing in private sector also started in and around Mumbai and Delhi. This later on came to be known as Real Estate Industry. As the private sector started playing a dominant role, the Government role has been reduced to that of providing housing to Economically Weaker Sections (EWS), Low Income Group (LIG), and other needy and specified classes. Housing has been largely a people' activity. Its contribution to housing ranged from 73 percent in Third Five-Year Plan to as high as 91 per cent in the Seventh Five year Plan. As per the report of the working group on finance for housing sector for the Eighth Plan, 80 per cent comes from private savings and non-formal sources of credit. The large proportion of houses provided by householders themselves constitutes the informal private sector.

## 4. HOUSING FINANCE – A GLOBAL PERSPECTIVE

Housing finance has been witnessing very substantial growth in the recent past, in many parts of the world including India. In fact, it has been identified as the driver for economic growth, as part of the retail lending boom. There have been certain favourable conditions for this phenomenon.

Many economies have met with fair degree of success in inflation management. Lower inflation (and lower interest rates as a consequence) provides the necessary environment for the growth of housing finance. In a liberalized and globalized environment, investment funds have been freely flowing across the globe.

With the recent spurt in the GDP growth across many countries, many people have been aspiring to realize their lifetime dream, namely owning a home.

Housing finance has prospered through the innovation application of technology. Transaction costs have crumbled, large number of transactions are now executed with speed and accuracy. Data collection processing and customer services have acquired efficiency through automation. Many housing finance products are used with ease and convenience in a superior IT environment. New delivery channels have come into use.

Many nations have been encouraging private sector initiatives in housing finance, with a view to meet the ever-growing demand. There are tax shelters for the borrowers. The legal environment has been gradually becoming lender friendly with rational foreclosure laws.

Lending institutions have been generally operating under conditions of financial stability with accent on rational pricing, relying essentially on credit scoring models. The securitization route has helped them lowering the regulatory capital even while handling higher volumes of loans, besides transfer of credit, interest rate and liquidity risks. The new Basel Accord stipulates lower regulatory capital for housing loans.

**Risk factors in housing finance**

Housing finance is a long term proposition involving many risks for the lenders, borrowers and even for the economy in general. While lenders need to manage interest rate risk, liquidity risk and credit risk, they have to cope with due diligence norms under the KYC system (Know Your Customer) when dealing with large number of individual borrowers. Legal risk cannot be underestimated as the legal system relating to the ownership on the basis of title deeds is not always uncomplicated. As housing finance is a long-term game, it requires proper Asset-Liability Management (ALM) strategy.

The borrowers also face interest rate risk, especially when they are locked in fixed rates when interest rates are falling and floating rates are raising. The awareness of the borrowers is not upto the desired level in many with regard to the interest rate sensitivity of the housing loans. Often their knowledge about the implications of certain mortgage contracts is inadequate. In the process, they are forced to bear disproportionate risks with regard to interest rates, while dealing with instruments like adjustable rate mortgage loans, negative amortization contracts etc.

The economy may also face certain risks if housing loans are not normatively disbursed. Housing prices could easily shoot up with credit driven demands. Asset bubbles could form, leading to bursts with grave consequences to the economy. Bankers, to their shock, notice rise in the loan to asset value ratio, resulting in default risk.

Refinancing and equity extraction strategies employed by lenders could result in wealth effect, under which there could be undesirable spurt in consumption and borrowing. The United States is a case in point, though the wealth effect there is more an equity price phenomenon than house price phenomenon. As housing finance occupies significant proportion of assets of the banks, any slow down in repayments due to systemic factors could adversely affect the banking system in general and economy in particular.

It is this context that there is a need for the regulators to follow sound risk management practices and to supervise housing finance trends and instruments on a real time basis.

**Financial Instruments**

Traditionally, housing finance is through term loans, backed by the security of the house, either on fixed rate or floating rate basis, generally with equated monthly installments. However, many innovative instruments have been introduced by the lenders, essentially driven by the competitive forces and consideration of customer convenience. There are flexible mortgages with variable repayments, floating rate loans with the facility of maturity extension if interest rates increase, variable payment mortgages, interest only loan, negative amortization loans etc.

Securitization process has given tremendous thrust to housing finance in countries like the US and those in Europe. It is a process of selling homogeneous loans for cash by the financing banks, to a Special Purpose Vehicle (SPV). The SPV in turn collects money by selling bonds, which have the security backing in the form of home mortgages. The bonds floated by the SPVs have a secondary market.[20]

**Housing Finance – The US Scenario**

In the US, Fannie Mae and Freddie Mac are the Principal GSEs that are instrumental in the high percentage of home ownership (above 70 per cent). These two enterprises enjoy implicit government guarantee and consequently raise long-term funds globally at low interest rates. Consequently, the interest rates on home mortgage loans have become relatively cheaper and affordable for middle and low

---

[20] KATURI NAGESWARA RAO. **Professional Banker.** (June 2006), p.17

income groups. Fixed rate mortgages are offered even for 30 year period, and there is the facility of refinancing the mortgages for the home owners. These two organizations, are instrumental in the securitization and development of a secondary markets for home loans. They have helped the US citizens to overcome the barriers of inadequate wealth and low credit quality in their effort to possess a home.

The long term fixed rate mortgages provide hedge against interest rate risk for the home loan borrowers, besides facilitating finance for consumption purpose.

**Housing Finance in Transition Economies**

Housing finance is not a flourishing activity in the transition economies for a variety of reasons. In many such countries financial stability has not been achieved to a significant extent. As a result, raising long-term funds and deploying them in the housing loans of long duration is proving to be difficult. Many countries in transition do not have a reliable legal system that confers property rights. Also laws relating to mortgages, foreclosures, etc., are not lender friendly. The banking system is also not strong and vibrant to promote on a massive scale housing finance.

These economies, therefore, have a long way to go in creating a suitable socio- economic environment for housing finance to prosper. In essence, these countries still need legal reforms to assure ownership rights and facilitate easy enforceability of mortgage rights in the event of default, a strong and well functioning institutional finance sector, a competitive environment to attract large funds on long-term basis.

### Housing Finance in Europe

Europe, known for strong and traditional banking, has a very advanced mortgage market as well. However, the foreclosure practices are not uniform. In Italy, for instance, a foreclosure will fructify in 120 months, whereas it takes just six months in Sweden and 9 months in Netherlands. Securitization route is employed by banks essentially to raise finance. Europe does not have any Government Sponsored Enterprises (GSEs) that caused revolution in the US, in the mortgage market. Also securitization in Europe is capital intensive and costly due to unfavorable treatment prescribed by EU directive for mortgage-based securities. The varying legal and fiscal complexities do not encourage large scale securitization.

### The Chinese Experience

China, the most populous state, with the highest GDP growth rate, is facing severe shortage of houses due to massive urbanization industrialization. While socialist China believed in total government involvement in providing housing, with limited property rights, modern day China has been attempting to increase private participation in housing. Chinese banks and institutions do not have any significant exposure to housing loans. This nation is yet to employ global practices like mortgage backed security bonds, securitization, etc., to popularize housing finance. It needs to tackle the challenge of raising long-term funds globally at cost effective rates and channeling them into mortgage loans through banks.

### Latin American situation

The Latin American countries do not have an efficient institutional mechanism for disbursing housing loans. This is mainly due to unsatisfactory legal *situation with regard to the property title deeds.* The mortgage lenders also experience many hurdles in enforcing eviction of defaulters and eventual sale of the house through legal recourse. Many citizens of the Latin American countries are generally very poor and hence cannot afford a home through the mortgage route. The volatile situation of interest rates is not conducive either for raising long-term capital resources or for lending mortgage loans.

State Mortgage Banks, which are engaged in the home loan activity are not very successful. They excessively rely on short-term compulsory savings and subsidized loan programs for the poor. These banks also suffer from political interference and macroeconomic instability, besides non-availability of long-term funds at reasonable interest rates. Even private sector housing market is not very active and efficient due to unsatisfactory legal system and unstable macroeconomic situation. The Latin American countries do not have a very good track record of managing inflation. Consequently, there are uncertainties in the interest rate scenario, which do not help in the development of an efficient mortgage market.

Private finance institutions have been raising long-term funds from external sources, in dollar terms. Consequently, there have been attempts to denominate the housing loan repayments also in dollars. This experiment, however, has not met with much success as the borrowers earn their income in local currencies and not in dollars.

Some of the Latin American countries have also been experimenting, though not with much success, with an inflation indexed credit system. There have been attempts to channelize private pension funds and insurance funds into the mortgage institutions. There is need to bring in new instruments like mortgage backed securities in the housing finance markets.

The discussion so far is made on the global position on housing finance and an attempt has been made to study the effectiveness of housing finance system in India and the role of the National housing and habitat policy in generating the suitable strategies for housing and the sustainable development of human settlements.

## 5. HOUSING FINANCE SYSTEM

Most countries have housing finance systems which are systematic institutional structures. These channel financial resources by way of mortgage loans, into housing investments. This forms the central core of housing finance which is supplemented by direct government programmes for low income people, mortgage insurance, interest subsidies and so on. In India the core is entirely lacking. Budgetary allocations that can be spared from alternative uses, are grudgingly allocated for housing programmes. While this is one method of financing housing, it is not the one to be recommended for a rapid, sustained and increasing flow of resources into housing. Secondly the powerful propensity of people to save specifically for housing purposes has been ignored. One of the major impediment towards developing a housing finance system is the lack of developed land in cities with adequate infrastructural facilities with clear tenurial rights.[21]

The role of the housing sector in the national economy has been largely ignored in India. A system of housing finance, though essential is only a primary pre-requisite of a national housing policy. A comprehensive policy would have to take

---

[21] CHAUDHARI I , **Housing Finance in India**, (Indian Institute of Public administration, New Delhi 1989),p.193

into account the required output of the building material industry, transport and delivery systems and general infrastructural development, such as the provisions of sewage, waste disposal, water and power. Nevertheless, the development of robust and efficient market in mortgages through a system of housing finance can contribute markedly to the development process by encouraging ancillary industries and environment development activities by local authorities and State Governments. The employment potential is enormous with its associated effects through the generation of effective demand.

A major additional benefit of a system of housing finance would be rapid and healthy development of the Indian capital market. By the issue of fresh instruments with which to raise funds, the channeling of additional resources raised by the mortgage markets and the development of a secondary mortgage market, the capital market as a whole can be broadened in smooth short term and long term aspects. Not only will resource be raised by the housing sector in the capital market, but also additional funds will flow through it from household savings raised specifically for housing purposes. Macro economic policy will become more meaningful as credit markets will respond more broadly to monetary policy thus carrying signals to much larger area of the national economy.[22]

Housing finance is a factor of production quite distinct from labour, materials and risk taking. The price of other factors involved in housing construction need to be paid mostly in cash at the time they are used. In the housing sector, finance serves the following vital purposes. Finance is needed for

---

[22] UNDERSTANDING INDIAN ECONOMY, **Profile on housing, Economic research and training foundation,** (Sowmya publications private Ltd., Vol II, Madras, 1982), p.17.

- Purchase and development of house sites, purchase of building material and for actual building of the structure.
- Meeting the annual charges consisting of the upkeep and maintenance expenses including rehabilation of kucha houses, taxes, interest and amortisation charges on capital and
- Covering risks involved in long-term housing investment.

The high level group set up by the Government of India in June 1986, under the chairmanship of Dr. C. Rangarajan, then Deputy Governor, Reserve Bank of India, classified the existing institutions into two broad segments, namely formal and informal.

According to the group the formal sector includes:

- Budgetary allocation by central and state governments including market borrowings.
- General financial institutions namely LIC, GIC, and its four subsidiaries the Providend fund and the commercial banks.
- Specialised Housing Finance institutions which include mainly the National Housing Bank, the Housing and Urban Development Corporation, Apex and Co-operative finance institutions in the public sector, Housing development finance companies set up in the private sector. The informal sector includes households and public and private sector employers providing housing loans to their employees.

In India, the existing housing finance system is dominated by a series of special and general financial institutions. Amongst them, HUDCO (Housing and

Urban Development Corporation) and HDFC (Housing Development Finance Corporation) are the specialized agencies, LIC (Life Insurance Corporation), GIC (General Insurance Corporation) and the commercial banks are the general ones. In terms of financial turnover, institutional sources account for only 10 per cent of total finance in the housing sector. Apart from this the informal sources of finance have a significant contribution to make. The formal sector institutions largely mobilize resources from general financial institutions leading to complex inter institutional flows.

**The National Urban Housing and Habitat Policy**

Shelter is one of the basic human needs just next to food and clothing. Need for a National Housing and Habitat Policy emerges from the growing requirements of shelter and related infrastructure. These requirements are growing in the context of rapid pace of urbanization, increasing migration from rural to urban centers in search of livelihood, mis-match between demand and supply of sites & services at affordable cost and inability of most new and poorer urban settlers to access formal land markets in urban areas due to high costs and their own lower incomes, leading to non-sustainable situation. This policy intends to promote sustainable development of habitat in the country, with a view to ensure equitable supply of land, shelter and services at affordable prices.[23]

---

[23] DRAFT, **National Urban Housing And Habitat Policy 2005**, (Ministry of Urban Employment and Poverty Alleviation, Govt. of India, 2005), p.3.

**Emergence of sustainable development**

In order to generate suitable strategies for housing and sustainable development of human settlements, this policy takes note of shelter conditions, access to services and opportunities for income and employment generation with particular reference to poor. This policy also takes into account the growth pattern of settlements, the investment promotion opportunities, environmental concerns, magnitude of slums and sub-standardhousing. This policy also examine the importance of sustainable urban structure which is able to

(i) absorb urban population with suitable access to shelter, services and employment

   opportunities and

(ii) also able to serve as service centre to their vast hinterland.

This policy re-affirms the importance of small and medium sized urban centres which have vast potential for future urban growth and also promoting a regional balance. These Centres, as per Census 2001, constitute only 31% of urban population, although they constitute over 90 per cent of cities and towns, being 3975. Our policy should be able to promote growth potential of these 3975 towns to divert rural to megacity/metro city migration and contain urban to urban migration in a desirable manner.

At the same time, this policy also focuses on in-situ urbanization of rural settlements so that connectivity at cluster level is improved for better provision of shelter, services and employment opportunities.

**Policies and Programmes**

This policy is in continuation of Public Sector interventions and related developments of human settlement sector in India during a period of last 15 years which began with the Economic Liberalization Policy of 1991, National Housing Policy 1994, National Housing & Habitat Policy, 1998 and follow up of 74th Constitution Amendment of 1992.These policy initiatives focused on increased role of the private sector, decentralization, development of fiscal incentives and concessions, accelerated flow of housing finance and promotion of environment-friendly, cost-effective and pro-poor technology

**Sources of Housing Finance**

Housing is a pressing problem in India. The problem becomes greater with time due to many factors like population growth, inflation and rapid urbanization.

**Formal Housing Finance System**

There are three formal sources of Housing Finance. These are:

a) Public and Private Institutions that have been set up specifically to finance housing activities.

b) Institutions catering to housing as well as to other sources such as Scheduled Commercial Banks, Life Insurance Corporation of India (LIC), General Insurance Corporation (GIC), Cooperative Banks, Land Development Banks etc. and

c) *Government, Public and Private agencies offering Providend Fund* Loans to their employees

Many among the public sector agencies obtain funds through bulk credit allocations from apex institutions or budgetary provisions of the Government. Their efforts to mobilize resources from the household sector or from the capital market have been marginal. Some of these do not advance loans to individuals and undertake mostly refinancing responsibilities. While commercial housing can be left in the hands of the private sector, the housing needs of the poor will have to be met by the government.[24] Significant changes have been brought about in their resource mobilization and credit disbursal policies in recent years. Let us now see the institutions providing housing finance.

## 6. INSTITUTIONS PROVIDING HOUSING FINANCE ONLY

### Housing and Urban Development Corporation

The Housing and Urban Development Corporation (HUDCO) was established in 1970 and is the largest Housing Finance agency in India. It was incorporated as a housing finance company on 24.4.1971 with an authorized capital of Rs.2500 crores.[25] Its specific objective is to improve the housing conditions of the low-income and houseless population. It provides financial support to public agencies like Housing Boards established by the State Development Authorities, Slum-clearance Boards,

Municipalities, Co-operatives etc., and not to individual borrowers. Funds have been advanced for infrastructure and urban development projects as well, but these constitute a small fraction of the total advances. Apart from the equity support of the

---

[24] ASSOCHAM RECOMMENDATIONS, **India Competing for the future.** (New Delhi), P.21.
[25] MANAGEMENT SERVICES WING, **"HUDCO in figures, India Habitat Centers,** (Lodhi Road, New Delhi, March 1999), p.29

Central Government received every year and its own earnings, HUDCO has been receiving confessional funds from GIC, the Unit Trust of India (UTI) and NHB and some International Agencies like World Bank etc. through the Government. It had received funds from HCs as well, till the early 1980s. The loans from UTI, however, carry the market rate of interest. HUDCO has been borrowing in the capital market through bonds, its public issue and private placement issue. It also mobilizes resources from Commercial Banks through the Statutory Liquidity Rate (SLR) Bonds, in accordance with the stipulations of RBI.

The major involvement of HUDCO has been in the financing of specific projects of Public Housing Agencies, undertaken on hire purchase basis. The rate of interest, period of repayment and the amount of loan advanced by it vary from scheme to scheme, depending on the income level of the beneficiaries. Recently, the thrust of HUDCO funding, and as a result, of Public Housing Agencies, has shifted from hire purchase to a self-financing system wherein the beneficiaries pay the full cost of the unit before, or at the time of occupation. The cooperative housing schemes under which individuals savings are mobilized on a large scale have also been encouraged. It has also initiated a few schemes to support Private Housing Agencies.

The lending activities of HUDCO during the Eighth Plan are expected to be primarily for land and infrastructure development and for EWS housing schemes. The enhancement of equity support from the Government and renewal of LIC funding for HUDCO are under active consideration by the Government. It may, however, be pointed out that the tax holiday enjoyed by HUDCO for the initial 20 years is over and that it is paying taxes before announcing dividends.

## National Housing Bank

The National Housing Bank (NHB) was established in 1988 as an apex institution with financial regulatory and development functions. It has received equity capital from RBI and confessional funds from LIC. RBI was made long-term operational funds available to it until 1991, at a highly subsidized rate. Being a statutory financial institution, it has raised resources directly from International Agencies. Funds have also been mobilized from the Commercial Banks through the SLR Bonds. Issue of Capital Bonds, which was yet another source of financing this has been discontinued since 1991

NHB functions as an apex institutional agency, providing financial assistance in the form of equity support and refinancing of loans to HFC, and not as a primary lender to individual borrowers. It extends its refinancing facility to Commercial and Co-operative Banks and subscribes to the Bonds and debentures of State Land Development Banks. It facilitates housing activities by providing short-term loans to housing agencies largely for "development and supply of land" and by facilitating the provision of long term loans to "individuals for buying a developed plot or undertaking house construction".

NHB has floated a contractual deposit scheme called "Housing Loan Account" (HLA), to mobilize resources from the household sector as was done by HDFC and a few State Housing Boards in the Country. As envisaged by NHB, an individual is required to open an HLA at a Scheduled Bank or a HFI which takes the responsibility of dealing with him or her on behalf of NHB. This would make the person eligible for a housing loan after three years. Savings, thus mobilized, would be transferred to NHB, which the latter would use for advancing loans to public housing agencies, contributing to equity capital of industries manufacturing building materials and refinancing the loans to individuals. Consequently, such individuals can purchase a house or developed plot, generally from a public agency on cash payment.

Under directions of NHB, loans are given to individuals by Commercial Banks and HFI for a maximum period of 15 years at rates of interest depending on the loan amounts. The rates determined at the time when NHB was established varied from a minimum of 10.5 per cent to a maximum of 14.5 per cent. The rate of interest of public agencies varied from 13 per cent to 15 per cent and a higher rate is proposed for time and cost over runs.

In accordance with its stipulations, NHB gives preference to agencies undertaking housing projects in rural areas and small and medium towns. The Public agencies are required to formulate projects by earmarking at least 50 per cent of the development land and 75 per cent of the plots, for small size plots, i.e., 60 $m^2$ or less. They are also required to reserve at least 75 per cent of built-up accommodation for housing units of 40 $m^2$ or less. The maximum plot size and built-up accommodation permitted are 200 $m^2$ and 120 $m^2$ respectively. The Housing Agencies give preference to HLA holders when allotting units or plots. The account holders can borrow under the NHB scheme even when they are not registered with any public agency under a Housing Scheme.

## Housing Development Finance Corporation

The Housing Development Finance Corporation (HDFC) was set up in 1976, to channel household savings as well as funds from the capital market into the housing sector. It has promoted ownership housing in urban areas through its retail lending policy. The HDFC has actively promoted new institutions for Housing Finance viz. the Gujarat Rural Housing Finance Corporation Limited with support from the International Finance Corporation, Washington, the Aga Khan fund for Economic Development Geneva, the Housing Promotion and Finance Corporation Limited with support from the State Bank of India and Capital Markets and Infrastructure Leasing and Financial Services Limited (supported by Canara Bank and UTI). In the case of the last three institutions, HDFC holds 20 per cent of their shares.

About 60 per cent of HDFC funds come from household deposits. These savings are mobilized through different deposit schemes, namely, the Loan Linked Deposit Scheme (currently not in operation), certificate for Deposit Scheme, Cumulative Interest Scheme, Home Savings Plan etc. The HDFC, like HUDCO, borrows from other financial institutions as well. However, unlike HUDCO a large part of its resources comes from the capital market through issue of Bonds and Shares. Like NHB, it borrows directly in the International market. These two, however are required to pay a higher interest rate than HUDCO, although the formers are covered against exchange rate fluctuations. HDFC has a track record of high growth and profitability and has consistency maintained sound financial position. The company has the distinction of being the first Indian Private Sector to raise funds under the

USAID, having guarantee programme. The amount raised under this programme was US $ 125 millions[26]

HDFC, which is the largest primary lending agency in the private sector, makes loans under various schemes to individuals, association of individuals, association of individuals, groups of individuals and individual members of Co-operative Societies. The Housing Finance Business accounts for 78 per cent of HDFC's total assets base of Rs.15,084 crores.[27] The rate of interest charged depends on the loan amount which, finally is determined by the repayment capacity of the borrower. In determining the repayment capacity, factors such as age, income, qualification, number of dependents, spouse's income, assets, liabilities, stability and continuity of income and savings history of the borrower are taken into consideration. The principle, generally adopted is that the instalment should not exceed 30 per cent of the monthly household income. The borrower can choose a repayment period in the range of 5 to 20 years, not exceeding the age of retirement of the loanee.

It is important to not that HDFC finances the construction of new residential units by an individual who or whose immediate family members do not own any dwelling unit. The security, which is the first mortgage of the property to be financed, is normally executed by way of deposit of title deed, which is essential for the loan. In case of property under construction, collateral or interim security is required, in terms of a Bank guarantee. Surrender of a Life Insurance Policy, the value of which is at least equal to the loan amount; guarantee from a sound and solvent guarantor; pledge of shares and such other investments that are deemed

---

[26] NAGARAJAN,V. **op. cit.** p.39.
[27] BUSINESS TODAY, **Journal,** (5th January, 2001), pp.80-81.

acceptable by HDFC. The title of the property should be clear, marketable, and free from all encumbrances. The insistence on security for the loan has been the major hurdle in the low-income household benefiting from these schemes.

**Apex Co-operatives at State Level and Afflicted Primary Societies**

Most States and Union Territories have apex Co-operative Housing Federation. These Federations mobilize resources from LIC, HUDCO, NHB and commercial Banks as loans and from their affiliated primary societies and State Governments as share capital. These basically finance the primary societies coming under their jurisdiction against first mortgage of the land or house. The pre-requisite of a loan from an apex co-operative society is, therefore possession of land.

It is not mandatory for the primary Co-operative Societies to approach an apex Co-operative Federation for funds. They can approach Private Financial Institutions such as HDFC for a loan. When a Primary Co-operative Society borrows from a Public Sector institution such as HUDCO, the loan amount is channeled through the apex Co-operative Housing Finance Society, which stands at a guarantor. The first mortgage documents in that case lies with the apex society.

**GENERAL FINANCING INSTITUTIONS PROVIDING HOUSING FINANCE**

**Commercial Banks and Co-operative Banks**

These banks mobilize over 40 per cent of the household sector saving. They provide housing loans (along with other loans) to individuals on terms fixed by RBI. The Commercial banks, the primary lending institutions, disbursed a negligible amount to the housing sector prior to their Nationalisation in 1969. After Nationalisation Savings Linked Housing Loans Scheme was introduced. This unfortunately did not make much impact on the housing scheme and remained basically as a deposit mobilization scheme. The main reason was difficulties in advancing loans against the mortgage of immovable property. It was legally difficult for the Banks to realize the loan amount in case of default. Acting upon the recommendations of working group set up by it. RBI made certain new provisions to increase the loan amount disbursed for housing by the Commercial banks in 1978. However, despite the new RBI stipulations, the allocation of funds for housing did not exceed 0.26 per cent during 1985-1987, against the working group projection of 0.5 per cent. This was largely due to the high risk and low volume of Business in the Housing Sector.

In 1989, the RBI stipulations were revised and the Commercial Banks were required to allocate 1.5 per cent of their incremental deposits in the previous year to housing. RBI also ordained that 30 per cent of this allocation would be for direct lending, half of which should be reserved for rural or semi-urban areas. Another 30 per cent would be for indirect lending and the remaining for buying Government guaranteed Bonds and debentures of HUDCO and NHB.

The linking of allocation for housing with the growth in Bank deposits led, in the initial years, to a substantial rise in the loan amount. The growth could not be maintained, as the bank deposit became a casuality in the 1990's. The percentage of bank deposits to total financial saving in the household sector declined from 45 in 1987-1988 to 39 in 1990-1991, since funds were attracted by more lucrative investments in the capital market.

Currently, the Government is considering the proposal to increase the allocation of incremental deposit for housing from 1.5 per cent to 3.0 per cent. A suitable insurance mechanism to protect mechanism to protect the Banks and HFIs against default in their long term lending for housing is also being envisaged. The restrictions on loan-disbursal pattern are also being liberalized to increase the commercial viability of the financial institutions.

## COOPERATIVE BANKS

Currently there exists a three tier system of Co-operative Systems i.e., State, District (including urban cooperative banks) and Village (primary affiliated credit societies). The Co-operative Banks in the rural areas have a wide network and can become excellent intermediaries for loan disbursal. Urban Cooperatives can bridge the gap between the formal and informal finance markets and thus can improve the accessibility to the poor for finance, including that for housing. It may be noted that State-Level apex banks are eligible for confessional finance for LIC.

In a similar fashion, the Land Development Banks also have their apex unit at the State level and affiliated Primary Land Development (mortgage) Banks at the Taluk level. These have expertise in evaluating and providing mortgage finance and they assist the Rural Housing Programmes.

## LIC Housing Finance Ltd

LIC Housing Finance Limited was promoted by Life Insurance Corporation, India's largest life insurance provider, to provide long-term housing finance to individuals and corporates for the purchase, construction, repair and renovation of new and existing flats and houses. It was incorporated under the Companies Act

1956 in Bombay on 19.06.1989[28] and went public in 1994. Today the company has emerged as the second largest housing finance company in India.

LIC Housing finance has grown every year since 1989. The company enjoys the full support of its parent, the insurance giant. As a result, the company's loans are usually, backed by a life insurance policy as a collateral security. In an indirect service to the community, the company also, finances doctors for the purchase and construction of clinics, nursing homes and diagnostic centers.

The Company possesses the widest marketing network of 97 offices and 100 camp offices across the expanse of the country. In 2001-02, the Company floated a 100 per cent subsidiary 'LICHFL Care Homes Limited' for the development of Assisted living community development for senior citizens on a commercial basis.

**Pension and Providend Funds**

About 11 per cent of all household financial savings go to Pension & Provident Fund. Currently a good portion of these funds is being utilized at budgetary resources of the Government through the regulatory provisions governing its investment. The contribution of P & PF to housing is currently by way of loans to its members. Since very few members have availed themselves of these loans for housing, only a small percentage of the total funds goes to the housing sector. The percentage share housing loans to P&PF collection had increased from 11 to 15 during 1983-1989. It felt sharply to 12 per cent due to the boom in the capital market,

---

[28] **Memorandum of Association and Articles of Association of LIC Housing Finance Limited,** (LIC. Publication, Bombay, 1989), p.1.

as noted above, but increased to 16 per cent in 1990-91. The Government is seriously considering the proposal to allocate 5 per cent of net accretion under P&PF for giving loans for buying securities of NHB/HFIs at the same interest rate as offered by the Government under the special scheme.

**Informal Housing Finance**

It was observed that much of the funds for house construction come from informal sources that include cash savings by households, loans and gifts from relatives, money-lenders, shop-keepers, landlords etc. The All India Debt and Investment Survey conducted by the National Sample Survey Organisation at the request of RBI in its 37th round had brought out useful information on the asset and debt structure of households in different asset categories as on 30th June, 1981. A few important characteristics of the urban households belonging to the bottom two categories for urban India as a whole are presented. It may be seen that poorest 14.4 per cent of the households (with maximum assets of Rs.1000) own, on average, assets worth Rs.373, of which only 10 per cent is in the form of land and building. The average figure for the next higher category with assets of Rs.1000-5000 and comprising 17.5 per cent of the urban households is Rs.2,746, of which 25 per cent is in land and building. The average for all urban households is Rs.40,573, of which 68 per cent is in land and building.

The average debt per urban household is Rs.1024 while that for the bottom two categories is only Rs.92 and Rs.292 respectively. Most of the loans taken by the households in these categories are for household expenditure. The average percentage of urban household loan used for housing is 60, as opposed to 15 and 30 for the bottom two categories, as may be seen in the detailed results of the National Saving Scheme (NSS). As much as 95 per cent of all loans taken by the households in the lowest asset category comes from informal sources. The corresponding percentage for the next higher category is 75 as compared with the national (urban) figure of 40 only. About 43 per cent of the households in the bottom two asset categories pay an interest rate of more than 20 per cent.

In this chapter it is highlighted that increase in population paved the way for housing problem. This chapter portrays that the housing has become important sector for the government over the years as it influences the national economy. It analyses the formal and informal sources of housing finance system to cater to finance housing activities. It induces the participation of government in housing in provision of housing finance, which is a major indicator of the growth of the nation. The following chapter elaborates the performance of the LIC Housing Finance Limited during the study period.

# PERFORMANCE ANALYSIS
## OF
*LIC HOUSING FINANCE LIMITED*

## CHAPTER V

## PERFORMANCE ANALYSIS OF LIC HOUSING FINANCE LTD

Housing is an important necessity of the human race and the Government is entitled to enact many financial measures towards the housing problem. It is apparently realized that to have a roof over one's head is very hard due to the heavy demand for housing. For this purpose many housing financial institutions were incorporated under the guidelines of National Housing Bank, an apex bank established by the Government of India as one of the measures taken to eradicate the problem of housing in India.

## GROWTH OF LIC IN THE FIELD OF HOUSING

In the beginning, the LIC was not significant in the field of housing as residential accommodation for large sections of the community mainly in urban areas, was not urgently required, but the investment in housing was so remunerative, that LIC itself could well undertake a large scale of programme in housing. It was true that LIC was engaged until then in setting up its own office buildings all over the country. The importance given to the life of the individuals necessitated the establishment of LIC and the importance of housing for such lives leads to the incorporation of LICHF with the control under LIC. In this chapter, the performance analysis of LIC Housing Finance Limited is attempted on two aspects.

1. Financial performance of LIC Housing Finance Ltd

2. Operational performance of LIC Housing Finance Ltd.

## LIC HOUSING FINANCE LIMITED

With the government finally recognizing the utmost importance of housing finance in a developing economy like India where a large part of one billion strong population is still deprived of decent housing, the housing finance industry has assumed all the more significance, and by now 400 entities, including housing finance companies and banks – nationalized foreign and as well as co-operative have entered the scene. One such prominent company in this field is LIC Housing Finance Ltd, a subsidiary of LIC of India.

It was established on 19th June 1989, under the Companies Act 1956. The company is recognized by National Housing Bank, the Apex institution in Housing Finance. Promoted by LIC of India the company became a public limited company in the year 1994. The establishment of LIC HFL has provided an impetus to housing finance. Its shares are listed on Bombay Stock Exchange, National Stock Exchange and Luxemberg Stock Exchange. Initially, the company used to meet its fund requirements mainly from LIC of India, but now it raises loans from commercial banks, issues the non-convertible debentures and also avails the refinance facility from NHB. The company has six regional offices, 115 area offices, 3695 Housing Loan Agents (HLAs), Direct Sale Agents (DSAs) and Home loan counselors as on March 31, 2006. It provides loans to individuals including NRI for the

i)    Purchase/Construction/extension, repairs and renovation of house;

ii)   Purchase of Plots;

iii)  Consumer durables; and

iv)     For construction or purchase of nursing homes and clinics to medical professionals.

It also sanctions loans to corporate bodies for the:

i)      Purchase, construction, repairs, renovation of office space; and

ii)     Construction of staff quarters for employees.

In addition to this LICHFL also gives loans to the builders for the development of housing projects. Various housing loans schemes of the company are:

- **Griha prakash** – Under this scheme, loan is available for construction/purchase of new/existing house flat, and extension to existing house flat. Amount of loan sanctioned ranges from Rs.25,000 to Rs.10,000,000.

- **Griha Tara** – Loan is available for construction/purchase of new/existing house flat, extension to existing house flat, and amount of loan granted ranges from Rs.25,000 to Rs.2,500,000.

- **Griha Jyoti** – Under this scheme, loan is granted for construction/purchase of new/existing house flat, extension to existing house flat and amount of loan ranges from Rs.25,000 to Rs.100,000.

- **Griha Shobha** – This scheme is open for NRIs only. Loan amount ranges from Rs.25,000 to Rs.1,00,000.

- **Griha Lakshmi** - Under this scheme, loan is available for construction/purchase of new/existing house flat, extension to existing house flat, and loan amount ranges from Rs.100,000 to 10,000,000.

- **Griha Sudhar** – Loan is available for repairs and renovation only, and loan amount sanctioned ranges from Rs.50,000 to Rs.1,000,000.

- **Sampurna Griha A** – Under this scheme loan is given to fresh borrowers for consumer durable items, and loan amount ranges between Rs.25,000 to Rs.200,000.

- **Sampurna Griha B** – Loan is available for existing borrowers with default free experience of at least one year for the purchase of consumer durable items. The amount of loan sanctioned ranges between Rs.25,000 to Rs.200,000.

- **Apna Chikitsalya** – Under this scheme, loan is given to the registered medical practitioners for having their own nursing homes/clinics/diagnostic center and the amount of loan sanctioned ranges from Rs.200,000 to Rs.5,000,000.

- **Griha Vikas** – Loan is available for personal and business needs and amount sanctioned ranges from Rs.100,000 to Rs.3,000,000.

## OBJECTIVES

The institution follows the policy laid down by the NHB. The main objectives are:

1. To achieve the aim of "**Shelter for homeless**".

2. To promote, a sound, healthy, viable and the cost effective housing finance system to cater to all segments of the population.

3. To establish a network of housing finance outlets to adequately serve different regions and different income groups.

4. To encourage the flow of credit and real sources to the small man first.

**FINANCIAL PERFORMANCE OF LICHFL**

The financial performance of a company is vital and plays a predominant role in assisting the management towards proper planning and establishment of policies. With the help of accounting information the performance of the organization can be properly evaluated. Many of the latest and most widely used tools are utilized in order to get proper and accurate information. From this information, the company is able to know its own strengths and weaknesses and it can then concentrate more on the progress of the company.

An overall financial performance for ten years of research period i.e. 1996-97 to 2005-2006 is given below in Table 5.1 Profit before tax and after tax stood at 87.73 crores and 63.38 crores in the year 1996-97and has grown by 16 per cent and 22.67 per cent compared to previous year. But the growth rate profit before tax and after tax has been considerably reduced during the year 1998-99 registered the decreasing growth to 11.95 percent and 13.26 percent from 23 per cent and 28 per cent in the year 1997-98. The financial results for the year 1999-2000 projected a profit before tax of 137.58 crores after writing off Rs.2.56 crores and provision of Rs.6.00 crores towards contingencies, doubtful loans, diminishing in investment and taking into account all expenses including depreciation of Rs.1.00 crore. After making provision for taxation of Rs.28.50 crores the net profit for the year is Rs.109.08 crores. Profit before tax has grown by 14 per cent and Profit after tax by 11.40 per cent in the year 2000-2001. During the year 2001-02 profit before tax and profit after tax stood at Rs.183.21 crores and 147.66 crores as against Rs.156.82 crores and Rs.121.52 respectively for the previous year thereby registering a growth of 16.83 per cent 21.51

per cent respectively. Profit before tax grew by 25.88 per cent and Profit After Tax by 21.98 per cent as compared to 2001 to 2002. But in the year 2003-04, Profit Before Tax has been reduced by 18.39 per cent and Profit after tax by 6.42 per cent as compared to 2002-03. There is a slight increase in Profit before tax by 8.53 per cent and decrease in Profit after tax and prior period items by 14.18 per cent. At the end of the research period i.e. 2005-06 Profit before tax and after tax stood at Rs.261.74 crores and Rs.208.57 crores registering the growth by 28.11 per cent and 45.12 per cent as compared to previous year.

## TABLE 5.1

### Financial Performance of LIC Housing Finance Limited

| Year | NPBT | NPAT | Total Income (Rupees in Crores) | Ratio of administrative expenses to housing loans (in %) | Dividend (in %) |
|------|------|------|------|------|------|
| 1996-97 | 87.73 | 63.38 | 411.70 | 0.60 | 20 |
| 1997-98 | 114.23 | 87.72 | 485.59 | 0.54 | 25 |
| 1998-99 | 129.74 | 101.14 | 561.60 | 0.48 | 30 |
| 1999-00 | 137.58 | 109.08 | 645.42 | 0.46 | 30 |
| 2000-01 | 156.82 | 121.52 | 745.55 | 0.51 | 40 |
| 2001-02 | 183.21 | 147.66 | 861.64 | 0.48 | 50 |
| 2002-03 | 230.67 | 178.97 | 1013.64 | 0.94 | 55 |
| 2003-04 | 188.24 | 167.47 | 985.38 | 0.68 | 50 |
| 2004-05 | 204.30 | 143.72 | 1048.27 | 0.69 | 50 |
| 2005-06 | 261.74 | 204.30 | 1268.83 | 0.61 | 60 |

Source: Annual Reports of LIC Housing Finance Limited

**Chart 5.1**

## FINANCIAL PERFORMANCE OF LIC HOUSING FINANCE LIMITED

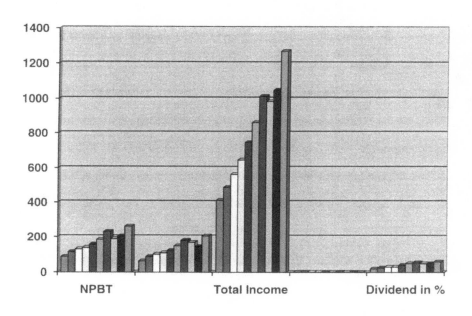

| ▣1996-97 | ▣1997-98 | □1998-99 | □1999-00 | ▣2000-01 |
| ▣2001-02 | ▣2002-03 | ▣2003-04 | ▣2004-05 | ▣2005-06 |

Chart 5.1 clearly brings out the trends in the financial performance of the LIC Housing Finance Limited during the research period 1996-97 to 2005-06. In the year 1996-97 the company earned a total income of Rs.411.70 crores and registered a growth of 22 per cent which has been increased to 1,268.83 crores in the year 2005-06 registering an increase of 20.78 per cent. The total income of the company has been tripled during the research period, which shows that the financial position of the company is favourable. The ratio of administrative expenses to the housing loans was 0.60 per cent in the year 1996-97, which has been reduced to 0.54 per cent, 0.48 per cent and 0.46 per cent in the year 1997-98, 1998-99 and 1999-2000 respectively. But there is a slight increase by 51 per cent in the year 2000-2001 and slight reduction in the year 2001-02 by 0.48 per cent. There has been a sudden increase in ratio of administrative expenses to housing loans by 0.94 per cent in the year 2002-03 and fall in 2003-04, 2004-05 and 2005-06 by 0.68 per cent, 0.69 per cent and 0.61 per cent respectively.

Considering the performance of the company during the year the directors will recommend the dividend per equity share. In the year 1996-97 the company recommend the dividend of 20 per cent, which rose to 25 per cent in the year 1997-98. A decade of service in the field of 'Housing Finance' to the borrowers LIC Housing Finance aggregated the dividend to 30 per cent in the year 1998-99 as against the previous year. In the year 1999-2000, the company declared a tax-free dividend of 5 per cent in addition to interim dividend of 25 per cent. There has been a continuous increase of dividend payment by 40 per cent to 55 per cent from the year

2000-01 to2002-03. But again in the year 2003-04 and 2004-05 it has been reduced to 50 per cent and rose to 60 per cent in the year 2005-06. The dividend payment has been tripled during the research period.

## FACTORS CONTRIBUTING TO FINANCIAL PERFORMANCE

The financial performance of the company is analysed by the following factors, to trace out the contribution of the factors to profitability. The factors are:

(1) Reserves

(2) Net Fixed Assets

(3) Total Assets

(4) Depreciation

A brief explanation of the above factors has been presented in the following lines to throw more light on their relative importance in the analysis

## RESERVES

Reserves represent total undistributed earnings of a company. It is an accumulation of profits over the years. Increase in reserves is an indication of higher profitability of the company.

A prudent company will not squander away all its profits; instead it would try to set aside a certain portion of its profits to some reserves in order to meet out any contingencies that might arise in future.

Efficient management of reserves is indispensable for the corporate excellence company. Thus reserves become important factors contributing to corporate excellence. So an attempt has been made to analyse the movement of reserves position of the LIC Housing Finance Limited. In nutshell, whether the reserves have actually improved or deteriorated over the years has been tested.

The company maintains a certain percentage of reserves yearly according to statutory provision. It is represented in the Table 5.2. On analyzing the trend of the reserves position of the LIC housing finance company, it can be stated that the company have registered an encouraging upward movement during the study period from 1996-97 to 2005-2006. It has been increased from 269.15 crores in the year 1996-97 to 1260.51

**TABLE 5.2**
**Trend of factors Contributing Profitability**

| Year | Reserves | Growth Rate (%) | Net Fixed Assets | Growth Rate (%) | Total Assets | Growth Rate (%) | Depreciation | Grow Ra (% |
|---|---|---|---|---|---|---|---|---|
| 1996-97 | 269.15 | - | 6.00 | - | 2883.47 | - | 3.05 | - |
| 1997-98 | 334.15 | 19.45 | 6.54 | 8.26 | 3387.93 | 14.89 | 3.95 | 22.7 |
| 1998-99 | 410.72 | 18.64 | 7.63 | 14.29 | 3994.71 | 15.19 | 3.67 | -7.0 |
| 1999-2000 | 493.95 | 16.85 | 8.37 | 8.84 | 4803.35 | 16.83 | 4.05 | 9.3 |
| 2000-2001 | 565.13 | 12.60 | 9.97 | 16.05 | 5905.95 | 18.67 | 5.04 | 19.6 |
| 2001-2002 | 663.65 | 14.85 | 15.70 | 36.50 | 6945.69 | 14.97 | 5.94 | 15.1 |
| 2002-2003 | 786.12 | 15.58 | 18.31 | 14.25 | 8265.72 | 15.97 | 6.92 | 14.1 |
| 2003-2004 | 886.33 | 11.31 | 23.69 | 22.71 | 10139.08 | 18.48 | 9.43 | 26.6 |
| 2004-2005 | 1110.05 | 20.15 | 24.75 | 4.28 | 12242.89 | 17.18 | 12.57 | 24.9 |
| 2005-2006 | 1260.51 | 11.94 | 24.24 | -2.06 | 15125.92 | 19.06 | 16.90 | 25.6 |

**Source: Annual Reports of LIC Housing Finance Limited**

crores in the year 2005-2006 which has been increased nearly five times over the period of ten years i.e. during the study period. It shows a mild decrease in the growth percentage of reserves position in the year 2000-2001 but has returned back to its increasing pace in the following years i.e. till 2004-05. The growth rate has been further gone down to 11.94 per cent in the year 2005 to 2006. Even though the reserves position shows an increasing trend, the growth rate of this increase is not uniform. It fluctuates widely over the years. This phenomenon justifies the fact that the company has in fact depleted the reserves over the years.

## NET FIXED ASSETS

Fixed or long-term assets are held permanently in the business. They are held for use in business and are not meant for sale.

"Fixed assets would include long-term investments and all non current assets. Fixed assets would generally form a major group in the manufacturing firms. Net Fixed Assets is obtained by subtracting the accumulated depreciation from the original cost of the fixed assets."

The Net Fixed Assets should be in an increasing pace envisaging the future development of the company. Improvement of net fixed assets, thus becomes an essential factor contributing to financial performance.

Table 5.2. reveals that the LIC housing finance company have a very good net fixed assets balance with a fixed growth rate. It has accumulated its net fixed assets over the years tremendously. During the period of study the LIC housing finance company has accumulated its net fixed assets in an encouraging way. It has been increased from 6 crores in the year 1996-97 to 24.75 crores in the year 2004-05 showing a regular increase till the year 2004-05. But there was a slight decrease to 24.24 crores in the year 2005-06 showing the negative growth at the end of the study period . A close observation of the trend of Net Fixed Asset would reveal that improvement of Net Fixed Assets is one of the important factors contributing to the profitability of the company.

## TOTAL ASSETS

Total assets includes net fixed assets and current assets. Fixed assets are held for a longer period while current assets held for a shorter period i.e. normally for a period of one year. Efficient and rigorous management of both fixed and current assets are necessary as it gives impetus to the company to outsmart its competitors. Inefficient management of total assets may cripple the future standings of the company. Efficient and effective management of total assets is an indispensable factor for the sound financial position of the company.

The analysis of total assets position in the table 5.2 over the period of study, it can be stated that there is efficient maintenance of total assets by the company. LIC Housing Finance Limited has accumulated its total assets uninterrupted over the study period. It has been increased from Rs.2883.47 crores in the year 1996-07 to 15125.92 in the year 2005-2006.

It has registered the fluctuating growth rate over the period of study. There was a sudden decrease in the growth rate in the year 2001-02 and 2002-03 but has returned back to its increasing in the following years.

## DEPRECIATION

"Depreciation is the diminution in the value of assets due to wear and tear or due to just passage of time. True profits of a business cannot be ascertained unless depreciation has been allowed for". The causes of depreciation are physical deterioration, economic factors, time factors and depletion. Amidst numerous depreciation policy, proper selection and pursuant of appropriate policy is essential to bring alacrity to the business. Efficient management of depreciation assures higher profitability. These reasons enable the depreciation to actively participate in the factors contributing to corporate excellence.

The depreciation has a great impact on the profitability of the company. The depreciation position of the LIC Housing Finance Limited has moved slowly over the years. It has also not registered improvement in a quick manner. It has been increased from 3.05 crores in the year 1996-97 to 16.00 crores in the year 2005-06, But it has been decreased in the year 1998-99 to 3.67 crores from 3.95 crores in the year 1997-98. There was a negative growth rate in the year 1998-1999. Thereafter, there was a fluctuation in the growth rate of the depreciation till the end of the study period.

## ACCOUNTING ANALYSIS

Analysis of LIC housing finance company has been done on the figures culled out from profit and loss account and balance sheet, in order to measure the profitability and its trend for the ten years period from 1996-97 to 2005-2006. The profitability of the company has been measured and analysed using ratio analysis. Ratios have been applied here as they give an accurate view of the performance of companies.

"A ratio is defined as "indicated quotient of two mathematical expressions and as the relationship between two or more things." Ratios are among the best known and most widely used tools of financial analysis.

They are very powerful analytical tools useful for measuring the performance of a Company. That is why, ratios are used as an index or yardstick for evaluating the profitability position of the company. The selection of appropriate ratios, the analysis of ten years and the interpretation of results on the basis of scrutiny of financial statements i.e. Profit and Loss Account and Balance Sheet help to overcome the general limitations of ratio analysis.

## RELATIONSHIP OF VARIABLES AND THE PROCESS OF ANALYSIS

Analysis of relationship between variables is the gist of ratio analysis. It becomes inevitable to compare some variables with the profits of the company in order to understand the profitability position of the company. As such the profitability analysis is carried out by establishing relationship between the profits of the company with the variables like capital employed, total assets etc. These variables are the major ingredients of the financial statements. Each category of these variable are further subdivided by analyzing the relationship of these variables with different stages of profit like Profit Before Tax(PBT), Profit After Tax(PAT) etc.

A brief explanation of the above variables has been presented in the following lines to throw more light on their relative importance in the analysis.

## BASED ON CAPITAL EMPLOYED

Capital employed is a combination of owner's and long-term lender's funds. It comprises net fixed assets plus current assets. Subtracting the accumulated depreciation from gross fixed assets derives the net fixed assets. Net current assets represents the difference between current assets and current liabilities.

It is vital to analyse the profitability in relation to capital employed, as the major contributories of funds i.e. owners and lenders will be interested in knowing the financial standings of the company. It is also worthwhile to calculate profitability in relation to owner's fund i.e. networth, as they are entitled not only to the residual profits. The tools used on the basis of capital employed are,

i)      Return on Equity(ROE)

ii)     Return on Net Capital Employed

iii)    Profit Before Tax to Capital Employed (PBT to CE)

## RETURN ON EQUITY

Generation of income for the benefit of the common shareholders is one of the primary reasons for operating a business firm. Return on Equity reflects the extent to which this objective has been accomplished. The operating efficiency of using the resources of owners can be measured by this tool. Not only the present shareholders but also the prospective shareholders are interested in this ratio to decide about the future investment in the company. The management team has a great responsibility of maximizing the owner's welfare.

"Return on Equity is calculated by dividing Profit After Tax (PAT) by Networth (NW). As the common or ordinary shareholders are entitled to the residual profits, Profits After Tax is taken as the base for calculating the return of them. The shareholders equity or networth includes paid-up share capital, share premium and reserves and surplus". That is

Return on Equity = Profit After Tax(PAT)
                   —————————————————
                   Net Worth(NW)

Looking at the analysis of return on equity in the Table 5.3 between 1996-97 to 2005-2006, it could be concluded that the company has registered a mixed performance during the study period. Return on equity has shown the increasing trend till 1998-99 i.e. 16.56per cent. But there is a sudden fall during the year 1999-2001. Again there is an increasing trend in return on equity. It is worth mentioning here that the company has not registered any negative growth during the study period of ten years in this yardstick used for analysis.

## RETURN ON NET CAPITAL EMPLOYED

Return on net capital employed can be used for measuring the success of the company in terms of profit. It can be used to show the efficiency of the business as a whole. For studying the economies of a particular line of business or for evaluating the efficiency of internal management net capital employed concept is more appropriate. Net capital employed consists of total assets of the business less its current liabilities. Income or net profits, for the purpose of computing net capital employed is profit should be what is earned by that capital. Therefore, the figure of profit, as used in the calculation of capital employed, is the net profit with adjustments made, if necessary. Return on Net Capital Employed will be calculated as follows:

Return on Net Capital Employed $=$ Adjusted Net Profit  x100

Net Capital Employed

From the given table 5.3 it is clear that company's money, which has been invested to obtain a return on their net capital employed is not much satisfactory as there is a fluctuating trend in the return on net capital employed during the study period of ten years i.e. 1996-97 to 2005-2006. It has been decreased from 2.23 per cent in the year 1996-97 to 1.42 percent in the year 2005-06. It is clear from the above analysis that the funds entrusted to the company have not been properly used since the return on net capital employed is not showing satisfactory growth rate.

## PROFIT BEFORE TAX TO CAPITAL EMPLOYED

Profit before tax to capital employed is one of the primary ratios applied to profitability analysis. Earnings before interest and tax includes, interest the fixed obligation of business enterprise. Comparing profit before tax to capital employed instead of earnings before interest and tax can derive more realistic results. Profit before tax refers to profit earned before tax but after interest. As the tax rate may vary year after year, exclusion of tax in the profit will help to analyse the profit actually earned with the capital employed.

Profit Before Tax to Capital Employed = $\dfrac{\text{Profit Before Tax}}{\text{Capital Employed}} \times 100$

The results of Profit Before Tax to Capital Employed has not been satisfactory during the study period with decreasing trend in the growth rate. It does not indicate an impressive performance. There has been increase in Profit Before Tax to Capital employed in the year 1997-98, but there is continuous decreasing trend over the period of study i.e. from 3.09 per cent in the year 1996-97 to 1.80 per cent in the year 2005-2006.

## TABLE 5.3.

## Financial Performance highlights of LIC Housing Finance Limited

| YEAR | RETURN ON EQUITY (ROE) (in percentage) | RETURN ON NET CAPITAL EMPLOYED (RONCE) (in percentage) | RETURN ON TOTAL ASSETS (ROTA) (in percentage) | RETURN ON SHAREHOLDE RS INVESTMENTS (ROSI) (in percentage) | EARNING PER SHARE (EPS) (in percentage) | PROFIT BEFORE TAX TO CAPITAL EMPLOYED (PBT to CE) (in percentage) | CURRENT RATIO (CR) |
|---|---|---|---|---|---|---|---|
| 1996-97 | 13.51 | 2.23 | 2.20 | 1.74 | 8.25 | 3.09 | 3.46 |
| 1997-98 | 16.43 | 2.67 | 2.59 | 2.80 | 11.45 | 3.47 | 2.53 |
| 1998-99 | 16.56 | 2.62 | 2.53 | 2.96 | 13.19 | 3.36 | 2.24 |
| 1999-00 | 15.72 | 2.35 | 2.27 | 3.40 | 14.13 | 2.95 | 2.75 |
| 2000-01 | 15.89 | 2.12 | 2.06 | 3.25 | 15.80 | 2.73 | 4.00 |
| 2001-02 | 17.10 | 2.19 | 2.13 | 3.23 | 19.69 | 2.70 | 3.84 |
| 2002-03 | 18.15 | 2.24 | 2.17 | 3.46 | 23.16 | 2.88 | 2.05 |
| 2003-04 | 13.23 | 1.70 | 1.65 | 3.53 | 21.69 | 1.91 | 1.86 |
| 2004-05 | 14.11 | 1.22 | 1.17 | -1.17 | 17.84 | 1.73 | 0.80 |
| 2005-06 | 12.78 | 1.42 | 1.35 | -0.53 | 24.56 | 1.80 | 1.32 |

**Source: Computed from Annual Reports of LIC Housing Finance LTD**

## RETURN ON TOTAL ASSETS (ROTA)

From the financial analyst point of view, the profitability of the firm can be analysed with reference to assets employed to earn a return. Here the profitability is analysed with reference to profits earned per rupee of investment made in the firm. Total assets represent pool of funds supplied by shareholders and lenders. Alternatively, total assets are calculated by adding net fixed assets and total current assets. It is analysed on the basis of Return on Total Assets

Return on Total Assets indicates the efficient utilization of assets in generating revenue. It is basically an index of earning power of the company. As capital investment decisions are made on the basis of this ratio, it occupies very important place in the analyst point of view. This ratio is attempting to measure the overall return the firm is generating on the amount of money invested in the business. Thus it measures the ability of the firm to earn income on its total assets base. Profit After Tax is divided by total assets for this measure. Profit after tax is there residual profits in the business, while total assets represents net fixed assets and total current assets.

Return on Total Assets = $\dfrac{\text{Profit After Tax}}{\text{Total Assets}}$ x 100

It is clear from the table 5.3 total assets have not been efficiently used in generating the revenue. Profit earning capacity of the LIC Housing Finance company from its total assets is not satisfactory over the period of ten years of study. There has been an increase in the return on total assets in the beginning of the study period. It has been increased from 2.20 per cent in the year 1996-97 to 2.59 per cent in the year 1997-98. But there has been a continuous decreasing trend over the period of study. Return on total assets has been decreased to 1.35 percent in the year 2005-06.

## RETURN ON SHAREHOLDERS INVESTMENT

Return on shareholder investment, also called Return on Proprietors funds is the ratio of net profit to proprietors funds as shown by the balance sheet, which are the same as total assets less liabilities. Shareholders investment includes all categories of share capital, capital reserves, all revenue reserves and accounts of appropriations profits. So far as profits are concerned, they are to be visualized from the viewpoint of the return to shareholders with the result that they should be arrived at after the payment of taxes and interest on long-term liabilities. This is so because this income alone would be available to the shareholders for dividends.

Return on Shareholders Investment $=$ $$\frac{\text{Net profit}}{\text{Shareholders Funds}}$$

Return on shareholders investment or return on capital is another effective measures of the profitableness of an enterprise. In fact this ratio is one of the most important relationships in financial performance analysis. The realization of a satisfactory net income is the major objective of a business and the ratio of net profit to shareholders, has been compared with the ratios for the study period of ten years from 1996-97 to 2005-2006 to determine whether the rate of return it attractive. In the beginning of the study period return on shareholders investment have been increased from 1.74 per cent in the year 1996-97 to 3.25 per cent in the year 2000-01. During these five years return on shareholders investment has been increasing. There has been a sudden decrease in the year to 3.23 per cent in the year 2001 to 2002,but again it reached 3.53 per cent in the year 2003 to 2004. The trend percentage of return on shareholders investment has been decreased to –0.53 per cent in the year 2005-2006 which shows that the profitability position is not favourable. In forming an opinion regarding the prospective earning capacity of an enterprise, it is no less significant to know about the character of directors and management, the probable demand for company's products, the supply of raw materials, industrial conditions and so on, over and above the information conveyed by the rate of return on capital.

# EARNING PER SHARE

The important aspect to be considered in the analysis of over-all profitability is the rate of return on equity capital, which relates the net profit available to equity shareholders to the number of outstanding equity shares in order to calculate earnings per equity share. For the purpose of calculating this return, net profits are arrived at after deducting the dividend due to preference shareholders, if any. Moreover, if preference shareholders have a right to participate further in the profits after a certain rate of dividend has been paid to equity shareholders, such participating dividend would also have to subtracted in order to arrive at profits due to equity shareholders.

Earnings per share = Net profits – Dividend due to preference shareholders

Number of Equity Shares

To gauge the performance of LIC Housing Finance Company in relation to profit earning capacity, a study of its earning per share is attempted. For this purpose the earning per share is presented in the Table 5.3. It could be seen that the earning per share has continuously increased from 8.25 in the year 1996-97 to 23.16 in the year 2001-02. One could infer the better performance of LIC Housing Finance Company. But for the year 2003-04 and 2004-05 the earning per share has gone down to 21.69 and 17.84 respectively. But it is interesting to note that the earning per share has gone up to 24.56 in the year 2005-2006. From the above analysis it is obvious that the earning per share from 2000-01 to till the end of the study period is much higher than the normal rate of earning per share, which is 15 per cent. Hence it may be said that LIC Housing Finance Limited has not been lagging behind others in earning profits.

## CURRENT RATIO

Current Ratio also called Working Capital Ratio, is the most widely used of all analytical devices based on the balance sheet. It matches the total current assets of the firm to its current liabilities. Current ratio is used as an indication of the company's ability to pay off its debts in the short term. It shows the amount of current assets the company has per rupee of current liabilities. It indicates the liquidity of current assets or the ability of a business to meet its maturing current obligations.

The minimum of 'two-to one ratio' is often referred to as a bankers rule of thumb standard of liquidity for a business. The quality of short term assets would be a pervasive factor in the interpretation of current ratios. Current ratio will be calculated as follows:

$$\text{Current Ratio} = \frac{\text{Current Assets}}{\text{Current Liabilities}}$$

From the Table 5.3 it has been analysed that the LIC Housing Finance Company will be able to pay off its current liabilities in full during the years 1996-97 to 2002-03.The current ratio during this period is higher than the ideal ratio 2:1. In the year 2003-04 to 2005-06 also the current ratio is nearing the ideal ratio. It has been reduced to 1.86:1,0.80:1 and 1.32:1 respectively during this period. During the ten years of period under study, in the first seven years from the liquidity position is very satisfactory especially during the year 2000-01 it has been doubled i.e. 4:1. It means that for every Re.1 worth of current liabilities, there are current assets worth

Rs.4. But in last three years of study the current ratio is not much favourable till 2004-05 but it has been slightly raised to 1.32:1 compared to previous year.

The above discussion reveals that the company exhibits a fluctuating trend in the profitability measures during the study period 1996-97 to 2005-06. The liquidity position of the company has been showing satisfactory results, which is showing the ideal ratio. The earning per share of the company during the study period is in favourable position from 2000-01 to till the end of the study period which is much higher than the normal rate of earning per share, which is 15 per cent. But the results of the other criteria are not satisfactory. It is to be mentioned here that the company has not incurred losses during any of the years covered under the study.

## OPERATIONAL PERFORMANCE OF LIC HOUSING FINANCE LIMITED

After analyzing the financial performance of the company, it will be worthwhile only when the operational performance of the company is discussed.

## SANCTIONS AND DISBURSEMENTS

Sanctions and disbursements represent the quality of loans and the total volume of business generated by the company. After a loanee submitted an application to the company, the credit was appraised and a sanction letter was issued. Once post-sanction formalities were completed the loan was disbursed. As a result, sanctions effectively represented the company's order book and the disbursement reflects effective deployment. Sanction marks the approval of the loan application, while the disbursement marks the movement of funds from the financial intermediary's account to that of the borrower.

At LICHFL, the sanctions and disbursements, functions have been segregated to enhanced effectiveness. While sanctions are done primarily in the company's backoffice, disbursements are done in the local offices. To enhance responsibility in line with increasing loan amounts, the company created layers with in its organizational hierarchy for sanctioning loans of increasing amounts, loans of Rs.60 lakhs and above were sanctioned only at the corporate level.

**Table 5.4**
**Sanctions of Loans**

| Year | Number | % of Growth | Amount (Rs in Crores) | % of Growth |
|---|---|---|---|---|
| 1996-97 | 39467 | - | 788.41 | - |
| 1997-98 | 38195 | -3.22 | 872.53 | 10.66 |
| 1998-99 | 41525 | 8.71 | 1087.96 | 24.69 |
| 1999-2000 | 49605 | 19.45 | 1433.58 | 31.76 |
| 2000-2001 | 54821 | 10.51 | 1743.69 | 21.63 |
| 2001-2002 | 62587 | 14.16 | 2109.85 | 20.99 |
| 2002-2003 | 84126 | 34.41 | 3593.45 | 70.32 |
| 2003-2004 | 91866 | 9.20 | 4068.57 | 13.22 |
| 2004-2005 | 83636 | (8.96) | 4415.05 | 8.52 |
| 2005-2006 | 81369 | (2.71) | 5027.28 | 13.87 |

**Source: Annual Reports of LICHFL**

Table 5.5
Disbursements of Loans

| Year | Number | % of Growth | Amount (Rs. in Crores) | % of Growth |
|------|--------|-------------|------------------------|-------------|
| 1996-97 | 37766 | - | 739.67 | - |
| 1997-98 | 36406 | -3.60 | 802.10 | 8.44 |
| 1998-99 | 38888 | 6.81 | 965.76 | 20.40 |
| 1999-2000 | 46672 | 20.01 | 1312.59 | 35.91 |
| 2000-2001 | 52258 | 11.96 | 1608.37 | 22.53 |
| 2001-2002 | 63927 | 22.32 | 1962.82 | 22.04 |
| 2002-2003 | 76663 | 19.92 | 3190.83 | 62.56 |
| 2003-2004 | 92827 | 21.08 | 3667.74 | 14.95 |
| 2004-2005 | 84387 | (9.09) | 4207.22 | 14.71 |
| 2005-2006 | 81708 | (3.17) | 4607.08 | 11.00 |

Source: Annual Reports LICHFL

Chart 5.2

SANCTIONS OF LOANS

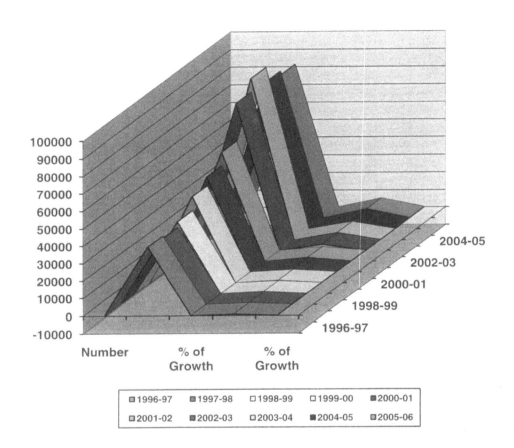

Chart 5.3

**DISBURSEMENTS OF LOANS**

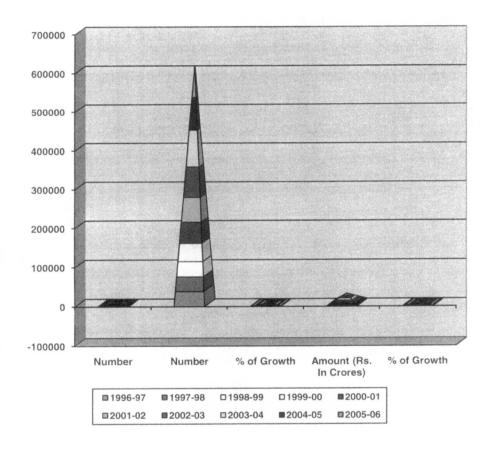

It is clear from the Table 5.4 and Table 5.5 that in the year 1996-97, the Company sanctioned 39467 loans for 788.41 crores and disbursed 37766 loans for Rs.739.67 crores. The Company has helped the borrowers to own 2.79 lakhs dwelling units as on 31$^{st}$ March 1997. The Company's sanction during the year 1997-1998 has been reduced to 38195 loans for Rs.872.53 crores i.e. growth rate of loans has came down to 3.22% from 4.41%. The disbursement rate also been reduced to 3.60% from 3.93% in 1996-97. During the year 2001-02 the company sanctioned 62,587 cases, a growth of 14.23% over the previous year. Disbursed loan cases increased by 25.49% to 63,927. Sanctioned loans increased 20.71% to Rs.2072.07 crores in 2001-02. Disbursements increased by 25.49% to Ra.2004.14 crores. Chart 5.2 clearly shows the trends in sanctions and disbursements during the research period.

Due to the use of strong technology, a rigorous validation and credit appraisal process that eliminate undesired cases, the disbursements to sanction ratio was at a strong 94 per cent. This indicates the company's speed in disbursements leading to superior customer satisfaction.

Despite the economic slowdown over the last few years, the company has consistently increased the quantum of its sanctions and disbursements during the year 2001-02. Disbursements have increased faster than sanctions, indicating a reduction in the company's response time. The disbursement to sanction percentage also improved to 93.6 per cent in 2001-02, because the company consciously focused on the individual segment, where the loan size was smaller and where sanctions & disbursements were transacted faster.

The Company sanctioned 84126 cases and disbursed 7663 individual loans during the year 2002-2003. Sanctioned loans increased by 70.32 per cent to Rs.3593.45 crores during the year while the disbursements increased by 62.56 per cent to Rs.3190.83 crores. The Sanctions and Disbursements during 1999-2000 to 2003-2004 have shown a healthy growth in the face of intense competition and a rate war. During 2003-2004 the total sanctions and disbursements of loans were Rs.4068.57 crores and Rs.3667.74 crores respectively as against Rs.3593.45 crores and Rs.3190.83 crores in the previous year. This constitutes 86.69 per cent of the total sanctions and 89.37 per cent of the total disbursements. During the year 2004-2005 the company sanctioned loans for Rs.4415.05 crores and disbursed loans for Rs.4207.22 crores. This constitutes 84.76 per cent of the total sanctions and 90.47 per cent of the total disbursements. In the year 2005-2006 sanctioning of loan amounts to Rs.5027.28 crores and increased by 13.87 per cent compared to previous year. The Company disbursed Rs.4670.08 crores which has been increased from 4207.22 crores in previous year 11.00% in the year 2005-2006.

At LICHFL the company is expected to strengthen its role in sanctions and disbursements the following initiatives:

1. Strengthen builder relations leading to exponential growth

2. Shrink the turn around time in sanctioning and disbursing funds

3. Disburse loans to borrowers directly from the back office.

Table 5.6

**Statistical Analysis for Loan Sanctioned and Disbursed**

| Variable | Results | Sanctioned | Disbursed |
|----------|---------|-----------|-----------|
| Sanctioned | Pearson Correlation | 1 | .999** |
|  | Sig. (2-tailed) | . | .000 |
|  | Sum of Squares and Cross products | 23142164.420 | 21301695.926 |
|  | Covariance | 2571351.602 | 2366855.103 |
|  | N | 10 | 10 |
| Disbursed | Pearson Correlation | .999** | 1 |
|  | Sig. (2-tailed) | .000 | . |
|  | Sum of Squares and Cross-products | 21301695.926 | 19649536.558 |
|  | Covariance | 2366855.103 | 2183281.840 |
|  | N | 10 | 10 |

** Correlation is significant at the 0.01 level (2-tailed).

The correlation coefficient between loan sanctioned and disbursed by the LICHFL is 0.999 and it is highly significant at one percent level. This show a high positive correlation between loans sanctioned and disbursed which is an indicator of the efficient loan management by the LICHFL.

**Region – wise Disbursements of Individual Loans**

The comparative position of six regions regarding the disbursements of individual loans is shown in the Table 5.7

TABLE 5.7
Region-wise Disbursements of Individual Loans

(Rs. in Lakhs)

| ear | South | South Central | Central | Eastern | Northern | Western | Overall Company |
|---|---|---|---|---|---|---|---|
| 996-97 | 18,824.99 | 18,056.10 | 5,632.82 | 2,549.21 | 7,251.01 | 14,518.71 | 66,842.84 |
| 997-98 | 21,939.47 | 20,510.26 | 6,182.24 | 2,929.19 | 8,763.88 | 16,606.12 | 76,931.16 |
| 998-99 | 29,515.50 | 22,634.55 | 8,064.91 | 4,125.77 | 10.511.99 | 19,639.90 | 94,492.62 |
| 999-00 | 42,854.66 | 29,577.45 | 10,491.83 | 6,967.06 | 13,045.50 | 25,569.73 | 128,506.23 |
| 000-01 | 56,033.17 | 32,905.19 | 11,843.32 | 9,475,76 | 16,873,02 | 32,572.58 | 159,703.04 |
| 001-02 | 67,816.40 | 46,188.49 | 12,549.23 | 12,373.38 | 24,098.44 | 31,853.93 | 194,879.87 |
| 002-03 | 89,291.12 | 65,460.61 | 17,099.69 | 14,758.00 | 39,608.76 | 47,910.97 | 274,129.15 |
| 003-04 | 111,823.00 | 77,396.03 | 28,319.00 | 25,336.00 | 59,865.00 | 64,048.00 | 366,786.00 |
| 004-05 | 115,025.00 | 88,878.00 | 30,911.00 | 37,044.00 | 93,156.00 | 55,708.00 | 420,722.00 |
| 005-06 | 123,198.00 | 94,974.00 | 33,634.00 | 47,072.00 | 114,595.00 | 53,534.00 | 460,708.00 |

Source: Conference Proceedings of Annual Meetings of Area Managers

Chart 5.4

## REGION WISE DISBURSEMENTS OF INDIVIDUAL LOANS

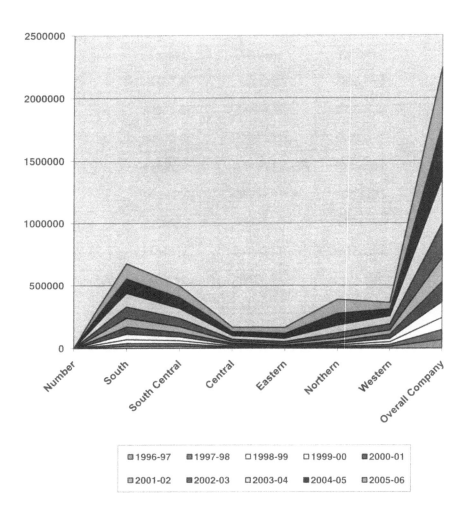

ova: Two-Factor for comparative position of six regions

arding the disbursements of loans

| UMMARY | Count | Sum | Average | Variance |
|---|---|---|---|---|
| Row 1 | 5 | 48007.85 | 9601.57 | 41667308 |
| Row 2 | 5 | 54991.69 | 10998.34 | 53805658 |
| Row 3 | 5 | 64977.12 | 12995.42 | 61552497 |
| Row 4 | 5 | 85651.57 | 17130.31 | 97550461 |
| Row 5 | 5 | 103669.9 | 20733.97 | 1.27E+08 |
| Row 6 | 5 | 127063.5 | 25412.69 | 2.03E+08 |
| Row 7 | 5 | 184838 | 36967.61 | 4.57E+08 |
| Row 8 | 5 | 254964 | 50992.81 | 5.3E+08 |
| Row 9 | 5 | 305697 | 61139.4 | 8.3E+08 |
| Row 10 | 5 | 343809 | 68761.8 | 1.18E+09 |
|  |  |  |  |  |
| Column 1 | 10 | 496580.7 | 49658.07 | 8.76E+08 |
| Column 2 | 10 | 164728 | 16472.8 | 1.12E+08 |
| Column 3 | 10 | 162630.4 | 16263.04 | 2.36E+08 |
| Column 4 | 10 | 387768.6 | 38776.86 | 1.47E+09 |
| Column 5 | 10 | 361961.9 | 36196.19 | 3.19E+08 |

ANOVA

| Source of Variation | SS | df | MS | F | P-value | F cri |
|---|---|---|---|---|---|---|
| Rows | 2.14E+10 | 9 | 2.38E+09 | 15.01692 | 9.55E-10 | 2.1526 |
| Columns | 8.63E+09 | 4 | 2.16E+09 | 13.62573 | 7.36E-07 | 2.6335 |
| Error | 5.7E+09 | 36 | 1.58E+08 | | | |
| Total | 3.57E+10 | 49 | | | | |

The ANOVA results given above shows that the F value for rows and columns are more than the critical value and hence it can be inferred that there is significant difference between the years and six regions regarding the disbursements of loans.

It is clear from the table 5.7 and the chart 5.4 that in case of southern region, the disbursements of individual loans were Rs.18,824.99 lakhs in 1996-97. Later it has risen to Rs.123,198 lakhs in 2005-06. The disbursement amount has risen from Rs.18,056.10 lakhs in 1996-97 to Rs. 94,974 lakhs in 2005-06 in the south central. Disbursement amount in the central region has increased from Rs.5,632.82 lakhs in 1996-97 to Rs.33,634 lakhs in 2005-06. In the case of Eastern region, the disbursement amount is showing the increasing trend from Rs.2,549.21 lakhs in 1996-97 to Rs.47,072 lakhs in 2005-06.

The data on Northern region also show the increase in disbursement of individual loans from Rs.7,261.01 lakhs in 1996-97 to Rs.114,595 lakhs in 2005-06. The data of the western region show the increase from Rs.14,518 lakhs in 1996-97 to

Rs.53,534 lakhs in 2005-06. Based on growth rate it is observed by analyzing the comparative position of disbursement of individual loans that the Eastern region has been at the top, followed by Northern region, Southern region, Central region, South Central region and Western region. It emerges from the analysis that the company schemes of individual loans are flourished well in the Eastern region during the study period.

## PORTFOLIO AMOUNT OR LOAN OUTSTANDING POSITION

Portfolio amount is a total outstanding loan of the company. Outstanding loans at the end can be obtained by adding outstanding loans at the beginning to the disbursements during the year and deducting the repayments during the year. The portfolio amount for all six regions for the study period 1996-97 to 2005-06 has been depicted in the Table 5.8 and shown in the chart 5.5 clearly.

Southern region is showing an increase in portfolio amount from Rs.64,447.57 lakhs in 1996-97 to Rs.414,332 lakhs in 2005-06. There is an increase from Rs.65,465 lakhs in 1996-97 to Rs.300,098 lakhs in 2005-06 in the South Central region. In the case of Central region, the data show increase from Rs.17,135.52 lakhs in 1996-97 to Rs.105,203 lakhs in 2005-06. Similarly, in the case of Eastern region, there is increase in portfolio amount from Rs.12,538.14 lakhs in 1996-97 to Rs.119,118 lakhs in 2005-06. This is increase in portfolio amount from Rs.23,987.70 lakhs in 1996-97 to 263,886 lakhs in 2005-06 in the Northern region . The data on Western region show the increasing trend in the portfolio amount from Rs.53,283.09 lakhs in 1996-97 to Rs.235,655 lakhs in 2005-06.

TABLE 5.8
Portfolio Amount of Six Regions

(Rupees in Lakhs)

| Year | South | South Central | Central | Eastern | Northern | Western | Overal Compa |
|------|-------|---------------|---------|---------|----------|---------|--------------|
| 1996-97 | 64,447.57 | 65,465.39 | 17,135.52 | 12,538.14 | 23,987.70 | 53,283.09 | 236,857 |
| 1997-98 | 79,663.47 | 78,681.38 | 21,326.79 | 13,919.90 | 30,512.24 | 63,622.66 | 287,726 |
| 1998-99 | 99,379.70 | 91,092.88 | 26,768.95 | 16,124.37 | 36,114.81 | 75,097.68 | 344,578 |
| 1999-00 | 128,289.72 | 106,059.39 | 33,185.42 | 20,653.14 | 42,384.05 | 89,830.23 | 420,401 |
| 2000-01 | 165,826.95 | 122,009.20 | 39,864.92 | 26,885.00 | 50,951.79 | 109,400.35 | 514,938 |
| 2001-02 | 199,979.70 | 143,300.14 | 45,712.16 | 34,984.41 | 63,017.48 | 129,545.57 | 616,239 |
| 2002-03 | 249,642.85 | 176,462.97 | 54,303.02 | 43,239.65 | 86,399.53 | 154,912.76 | 764,960 |
| 2003-04 | 303,849.15 | 210,246.11 | 70,018.01 | 59,991.21 | 122,600.5 | 190,175.78 | 956,880 |
| 2004-05 | 355,900.75 | 251,808.58 | 87,409.15 | 86,231.11 | 185,227.70 | 215,569.66 | 1,182,14 |
| 2005-06 | 414,332.00 | 300,098.00 | 105,203.00 | 119,118.00 | 263,886.00 | 235,655.00 | 1,439,85 |

Source: Conference proceedings of Annual meetings of area managers

Chart 5.5

## PORT FOLIO AMOUNT OF SIX REGIONS

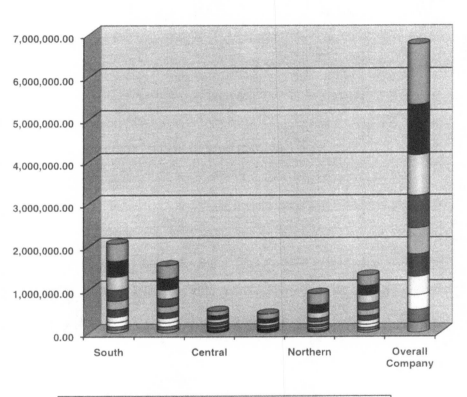

The overall growth rate of company stands at 22.19%. The comparative analysis in case of portfolio amount states that the Northern region is having the highest growth rate followed by Eastern, Southern, Central, Western and South Central regions. One of the possible explanations of this phenomenon might be the increasing compound annual growth rate of disbursements over the years, and other might be the delay in the repayments of loan amount. So far as the disbursements are concerned, the increase in the growth rates indicate the positive development on the part of the company as a whole, but regarding the delay in the repayments, there is a need to take appropriate steps for recovery.

## REGIONWISE POSITION OF DEFAULTS

The position of defaults from 1996-97 to 2005 -06 is shown in the Table 5.9 Southern region is showing the increase in defaults amount from Rs.1044.44 lakhs in 1996-97 to Rs.4,328 lakhs in 2005-2006. In respect of defaults amount, the position of South Central region is also the same. The data show an increase from Rs.951.32 lakhs in 1996-97 to Rs.4.039.34 lakhs in 2005-2006. Similarly, in case of Central region, there is an increase from Rs.334.31 lakhs in 1996-97 to Rs.1,431.07 lakhs in 2005-2006.

The data on Eastern region show an increase in defaults from Rs.577.56 lakhs in 1996-97 to Rs.1,793.76 lakhs in 2005-06. There is increase in defaults in the Northern region, amounting from Rs.410.41 lakhs in 1996-97 to Rs.875.64 lakhs in 2005-06. Similarly, in the case of Western region, there is increase from Rs.436.81 lakhs in 1996-97 to Rs.6,953.75 lakhs in 2005-06.

**TABLE 5.9**
**Region-wise Position of Defaults**

(Rupees in Lakhs)

| Year | South | South Central | Central | Eastern | Northern | Western | Overall Company |
|---|---|---|---|---|---|---|---|
| 1996-97 | 1,044.44 | 951.32 | 334.31 | 577.56 | 410.41 | 436.81 | 3,754.85 |
| 1997-98 | 1,230.53 | 1,172.44 | 403.68 | 760.71 | 454.98 | 529.21 | 4,551.55 |
| 1998-99 | 1,309,97 | 1,462.29 | 480.08 | 963.31 | 526.47 | 788.73 | 5,530.85 |
| 1999-00 | 1,276.79 | 1,727.72 | 592.64 | 1,110.59 | 606.17 | 944.95 | 6,258.91 |
| 2000-01 | 1,884.74 | 2,381.54 | 772.64 | 1,386.71 | 740.41 | 1,400.62 | 8,566.66 |
| 2001-02 | 2,695.89 | 2,968.38 | 1,005.93 | 1,584.87 | 843.33 | 2,424.40 | 11,522.80 |
| 2002-03 | 3,521.90 | 3,444.75 | 1,156.33 | 1,857.13 | 935.79 | 3,418.50 | 14,334.40 |
| 2003-04 | 3,637.68 | 3,592.64 | 1,211.10 | 1,697.02 | 958.87 | 3,832.31 | 14,924.16 |
| 2004-05 | 4,218.68 | 3,938.85 | 1,383.94 | 1,734.96 | 953.18 | 5,254.20 | 17,483.81 |
| 2005-06 | 4,328.00 | 4,039.34 | 1,431.07 | 1,793.76 | 875.64 | 6,953.75 | 19,422.00 |

Source: Conference Proceeedings of Area Managers

Chart 5.6

REGION WISE POSITION OF DEFAULTS

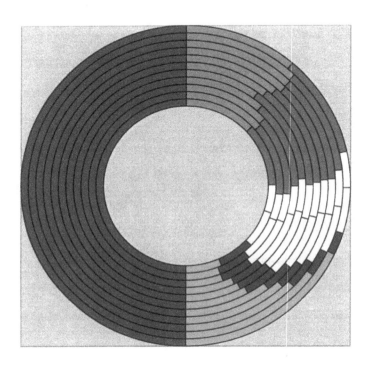

Calculating the rate of defaults amount to portfolio amount also makes intra region comparison. Table.5.10 and chart 5.7 clearly portrays that in case of Northern region, there is remarkable change in the ratio of default to portfolio amount. Ratio of defaults to portfolio amount is showing downward trend for all the years except 2000-01, indicating the positive development. There is almost 75.12 per cent decrease in the ratio in 2004-05, as compared to 1996-97 showing that the northern region is paying more attention to improve its recovery mechanisms as well as loan appraisal system.

In the case of Southern region, we observe that for the first four year the ratio depicts the declining trend. Again for the next three years i.e., from 2000-01 to 2002-03, there is continuous increase in the percentage of defaults to portfolio amount. From 2003-04 onwards, there is decrease in the ratio.

The position of South Central region is very much different in this context. The ratio of default to portfolio is increasing continuously up to 2001-02. There has been a declining trend till the year 2005-06. It means that the adequate attention is not being paid to control the defaults as well as to implement the better recovery mechanisms. The ratio of default to portfolio amount is showing declining trend from 1996-97 to 1999-2000 in the case of Central region. However, for 2000-01 and 2001-02, the ratio has been increasing. There is decrease in the ratio. So we observe fluctuations in trend of this ratio in case of central region, which is clearly given in the chart 5.7.

TABLE 5.10
Percentage of Defaults to Portfolio Amount

| Year | South | South Central | Central | Eastern | Northern | Western | Overall Company |
|------|-------|---------------|---------|---------|----------|---------|-----------------|
| 1996-97 | 1.62 | 1.45 | 1.95 | 4.61 | 1.71 | 0.82 | 1.58 |
| 1997-98 | 1.54 | 1.49 | 1.89 | 5.46 | 1.49 | 0.83 | 1.58 |
| 1998-99 | 1.32 | 1.60 | 1.79 | 5.97 | 1.46 | 1.05 | 1.60 |
| 1999-00 | 0.99 | 1.63 | 1.78 | 5.38 | 1.43 | 1.05 | 1.49 |
| 2000-01 | 1.14 | 1.95 | 1.94 | 5.16 | 1.45 | 1.28 | 166.00 |
| 2001-02 | 134.00 | 2.07 | 2.02 | 4.57 | 1.34 | 1.87 | 1.87 |
| 2002-03 | 1.41 | 1.95 | 2.13 | 4.29 | 1.08 | 2.21 | 1.87 |
| 2003-04 | 1.19 | 1.71 | 1.73 | 2.83 | 0.78 | 2.01 | 1.56 |
| 2004-05 | 1.18 | 1.56 | 1.58 | 2.01 | 0.51 | 2.44 | 1.48 |
| 2005-06 | 1.04 | 1.34 | 1.36 | 1.50 | 0.33 | 2.95 | 1.35 |

Source: Computed

Chart 5.7

# PERCENTAGE OF DEFAULTS TO PORTFOLIO AMOUNT

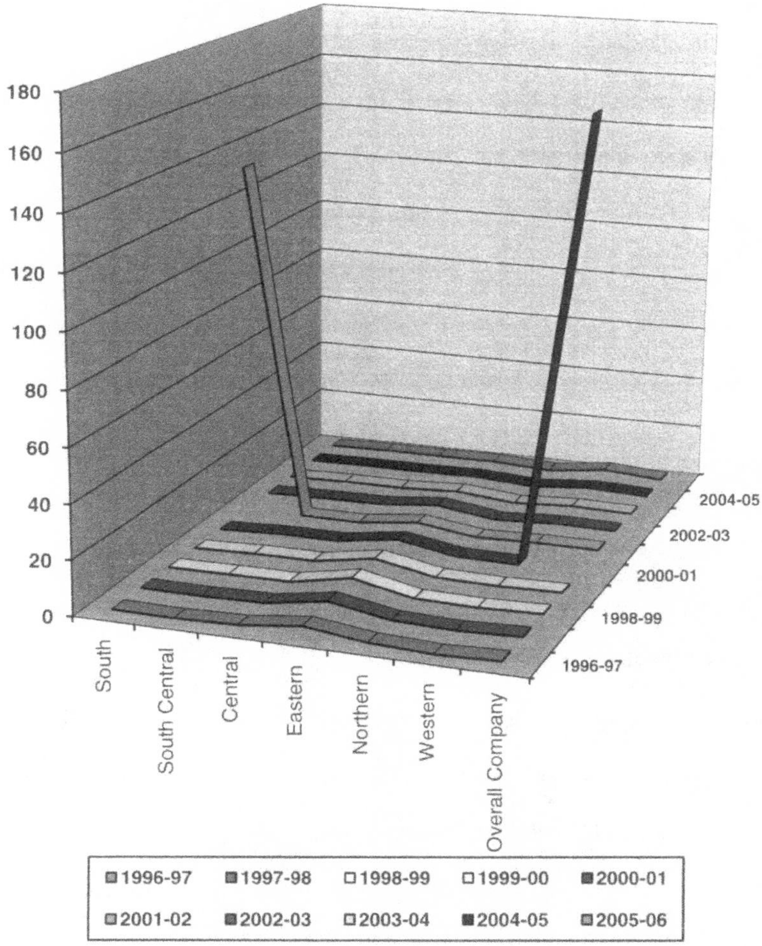

| ▣1996-97 | ▣1997-98 | ▢1998-99 | ▢1999-00 | ▪2000-01 |
| ▣2001-02 | ▪2002-03 | ▢2003-04 | ▪2004-05 | ▣2005-06 |

## PERCENTAGE OF DEFAULTS TO PORTFOLIO AMOUNT

The ratio in the Eastern region is increasing for first four years i.e., from 1996-97 to 1998-99. From 1999-2000 onwards, there has been continuous decrease in the ratio of defaults to portfolio amount. There are also fluctuations in the trend of ratio in the case of Western region. In 1996-97, a decrease in the ratio has been observed and from 1997-98 to 2002-03, there is an increase in the ratio. The ratio becomes consistent for two years i.e., in 1998-99 and 1999-2000. In 2003-04, there is a decrease in the ratio, but again for the next year, the ratio of defaults in portfolio amount has increased. While analyzing the overall position of the company in this context, a decrease of 10.30% has been observed in this ratio, but we observe that the portfolio amount and defaults are growing almost at the same rate. This suggests taking the appropriate actions to control the defaults.

From the above analysis on the basis of compound growth rates, it may be concluded that the Eastern region ranks first in the disbursement of individual loans. It means the company's schemes of housing loans are flourishing well in this region. So far as portfolio amount and default figure are concerned, the Northern region occupies the first rank. This region has the lowest compound growth rate of defaults as compared to other regions. It means that the credit analysis, appraisal and management of this region are better. While analyzing the overall position of the company, it emerges that there is a need to bring down the default figures for its survival. Serious actions have not been taken up by some of the area officers such as western region, South Central region and Southern region at this front, and hence, it results into huge increase in defaults. More attention is being paid by the area managers of these regions to achieve the disbursements targets than to introduce the better default recovery mechanisms.

EVALUATION OF LIC HOUSING
FINANCE LIMITED BY THE SAMPLE
BENEFICIARIES IN CHENNAI

# CHAPTER VI

# EVALUATION OF LIC HOUSING FINANCE LIMITED BY THE SAMPLE BENEFICIARIES IN CHENNAI

The demand for houses goes up as the people move towards urban areas for job, education and to lead a better life in the city. This accentuates the demand for new houses in the urban area. These migrated people choose to purchase new house instead of seeking a rented house. Not all of them have sufficient money to invest in their new house and they go for housing finance from various institutions. Further, housing finance is boon for removing houselessness in a country. Housing finance poses big problem due to overcrowding of borrowers and the policies of these lending agencies. In this chapter, opinion of the housing loan borrowers of the LIC Housing Finance Limited on the following aspects.

1. Identification.

2. Socio-Economic and Cultural Status.

3. LIC Housing Finance Limited and Loans.

4. Repayment of Loan.

5. Opinion of the Borrowers.

6. Problems Faced by Borrowers.

**IDENTIFICATION**

In the identification of the beneficiaries of LIC Housing Finance Limited, age, sex, community, religion and marital status are analysed with the primary data collected from the sample respondents.

Age

Age in different years and the number of borrowers in each age is an important indicator of borrower's status. Table 6.1 shows the actual age level of sample respondents from LIC Housing Finance Limited in Chennai.

Table 6.1
Age Wise Distribution of the Sample Respondents in Chennai

| Sl.No | Age in years | Frequency | Percent | Valid Percent | Cumulative Percent |
|-------|--------------|-----------|---------|---------------|--------------------|
| 1 | 22 | 2 | 0.7 | 0.7 | 0.7 |
| 2 | 25 | 2 | 0.7 | 0.7 | 1.3 |
| 3 | 26 | 3 | 1.0 | 1.0 | 2.3 |
| 4 | 27 | 1 | 0.3 | 0.3 | 2.7 |
| 5 | 28 | 3 | 1.0 | 1.0 | 3.7 |
| 6 | 29 | 7 | 2.3 | 2.3 | 6.0 |
| 7 | 30 | 4 | 1.3 | 1.3 | 7.3 |
| 8 | 31 | 9 | 3.0 | 3.0 | 10.3 |
| 9 | 32 | 15 | 5.0 | 5.0 | 15.3 |
| 10 | 33 | 9 | 3.0 | 3.0 | 18.3 |
| 11 | 34 | 9 | 3.0 | 3.0 | 21.3 |
| 12 | 35 | 37 | 12.3 | 12.3 | 33.7 |
| 13 | 36 | 10 | 3.3 | 3.3 | 37.0 |
| 14 | 37 | 41 | 13.7 | 13.7 | 50.7 |
| 15 | 38 | 29 | 9.7 | 9.7 | 60.3 |
| 16 | 39 | 24 | 8.0 | 8.0 | 68.3 |
| 17 | 40 | 29 | 9.7 | 9.7 | 78.0 |
| 18 | 41 | 12 | 4.0 | 4.0 | 82.0 |
| 19 | 42 | 13 | 4.3 | 4.3 | 86.3 |
| 20 | 43 | 4 | 1.3 | 1.3 | 87.7 |
| 21 | 44 | 3 | 1.0 | 1.0 | 88.7 |
| 22 | 45 | 10 | 3.3 | 3.3 | 92.0 |
| 23 | 46 | 2 | 0.7 | 0.7 | 92.7 |
| 24 | 47 | 5 | 1.7 | 1.7 | 94.3 |
| 25 | 48 | 2 | 0.7 | 0.7 | 95.0 |
| 26 | 49 | 2 | 0.7 | 0.7 | 95.7 |
| 27 | 50 | 4 | 1.3 | 1.3 | 97.0 |
| 28 | 52 | 2 | 0.7 | 0.7 | 97.7 |
| 29 | 53 | 1 | 0.3 | 0.3 | 98.0 |
| 30 | 54 | 2 | 0.7 | 0.7 | 98.7 |
| 31 | 55 | 1 | 0.3 | 0.3 | 99.0 |
| 32 | 58 | 3 | 0.9 | 0.9 | 100.0 |
| | Total | 300 | 100.0 | 100.0 | |

Source: Computed from primary data

Table 6.1 portrays that of the 300 sample respondents 41 of them are 37 years of age, 37 of them in 35 years of age, 29 of them in 38 and 40 years of age, 24 of them in 39 years, 13 of them in 42 years of age, 15 of them in 32 years of age, 12 of them in 41 years of age and 10 of them in 45 years of age. The number of sample respondents in 22 to 31 years and 46 to 58 years of age are less than 9 but more than one. Chart 6.1 gives the age and borrowers details.

SEX

**Table 6.2**
**Sex Wise Distribution of the Sample Respondents in Chennai**

| Sl.No | Sex | Frequency | Percent | Valid Percent | Cumulative Percent |
|-------|------|-----------|---------|---------------|--------------------|
| 1 | Male | 260 | 86.7 | 86.7 | 86.7 |
| 2 | Female | 40 | 13.3 | 13.3 | 100.0 |
| | Total | 300 | 100.0 | 100.0 | |

**Source: Computed from primary data**

Table 6.2 shows that 86.7 percent of the sample borrowers are male and 13.3 percent of them are female. The male borrowers are more because of the male employment is more than the female employment in the study area.

## Chart 6.1

## AGE WISE DISTRIBUTION OF THE SAMPLE RESPONDENTS IN CHENNAI

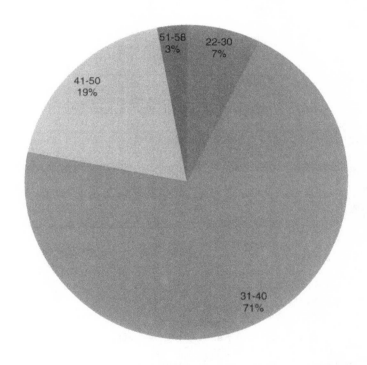

COMMUNITY

### Table 6.3
### Community Wise Distribution of the Sample Respondents in Chennai

| Sl.No | Community | Frequency | Percent | Valid Percent | Cumulative Percent |
|---|---|---|---|---|---|
| 1 | ST | 3 | 1.0 | 1.0 | 1.0 |
| 2 | SC | 22 | 7.3 | 7.3 | 8.3 |
| 3 | MBC | 99 | 33.0 | 33.0 | 41.3 |
| 4 | BC | 131 | 43.7 | 43.7 | 85.0 |
| 5 | OC | 45 | 15.0 | 15.0 | 100.0 |
| | Total | 300 | 100.0 | 100.0 | |

Source: Computed from primary data

As found in Table 6.3 about 43.7 percent are Backward Class (BC), 33 percent are Most Backward Class (MBC), 15 percent are Other Castes (OC), 7.3 percent are Scheduled Castes (SC) and the rest of one percent are Scheduled Tribes (ST).

RELIGION

### Table 6.4
### Religion Details of the Sample Respondents in Chennai

| Sl.No | Religion | Frequency | Percent | Valid Percent | Cumulative Percent |
|---|---|---|---|---|---|
| 1 | Hindu | 256 | 85.3 | 85.3 | 85.3 |
| 2 | Muslim | 8 | 2.7 | 2.7 | 88.0 |
| 3 | Christian | 31 | 10.3 | 10.3 | 98.3 |
| 4 | Others | 5 | 1.6 | 1.6 | 100.0 |
| | Total | 300 | 100.0 | 100.0 | |

Source: Computed from primary data

Table 6.4 portrays that among the borrowers 85.3 percent are Hindus, 10.3 percent are Christians, 2.7 percent are Muslims and 1.6 percent are others like Jains etc. The data shows the borrowing of housing loan by sample households in all the major religions.

## MARITAL STATUS

### Table 6.5
### Marital Status of the Sample Respondents in Chennai

| Sl.No | Marital | Frequency | Percent | Valid Percent | Cumulative Percent |
|-------|---------|-----------|---------|---------------|--------------------|
| 1 | Single | 14 | 4.7 | 4.7 | 4.7 |
| 2 | Married | 286 | 95.3 | 95.3 | 100.0 |
|  | Total | 300 | 100.0 | 100.0 |  |

**Source: Computed from primary data**

Among the home loan borrowers 95.3 percent are married and 4.7 percent are single. The married number is more as they need home loan earnestly.

## SOCIO-ECONOMIC AND CULTURAL STATUS

Education, occupation and type of family are the important socio-economic and cultural factors are discussed below.

## EDUCATION

### Table 6.6
### Education level of the Sample Respondents in Chennai

| Sl.No | Education | Frequency | Percent | Valid Percent | Cumulative Percent |
|-------|-----------|-----------|---------|---------------|--------------------|
| 1 | Illiterate | 4 | 1.3 | 1.3 | 1.3 |
| 2 | Primary | 2 | 0.7 | 0.7 | 2.0 |
| 3 | Elementary | 3 | 1.0 | 1.0 | 3.0 |
| 4 | High School | 34 | 11.3 | 11.3 | 14.3 |
| 5 | Higher Secondary | 40 | 13.3 | 13.3 | 27.7 |
| 6 | College | 123 | 41.0 | 41.0 | 68.7 |
| 7 | Professional | 92 | 30.7 | 30.7 | 99.3 |
| 8 | Technical | 2 | 0.7 | 0.7 | 100.0 |
|  | Total | 300 | 100.0 | 100.0 |  |

**Source: Computed from primary data**

Table 6.6 shows that educated sample respondents are more (98.7 percent) than illiterates (1.3 percent). Of the educated, sample respondents studied college level (41 percent) is more than professionals (30.7 percent), higher secondary (13.3 percent) and high school (11.3 percent). Sample respondents studied primary school level, technical and elementary school is less than one percent of the total sample population. Chart 6.2 gives the educational details of the sample population in the study area.

**OCCUPATION**

Table 6.7
Occupation level of the Sample Respondents in Chennai

| Sl.No | Occupation | Frequency | Percent | Valid Percent | Cumulative Percent |
|-------|-----------|-----------|---------|---------------|--------------------|
| 1 | Government | 62 | 20.7 | 20.7 | 20.7 |
| 2 | Private | 97 | 32.3 | 32.3 | 53.0 |
| 3 | Professional | 45 | 15.0 | 15.0 | 68.0 |
| 4 | Business | 61 | 20.3 | 20.3 | 88.3 |
| 5 | Skilled Labour | 20 | 6.7 | 6.7 | 95.0 |
| 6 | Self Employed | 15 | 5.0 | 5.0 | 100.0 |
| | Total | 300 | 100.0 | 100.0 | |

Source: Computed from primary data

**Chart 6.2**

**Education level of the Sample Respondents in Chennai**

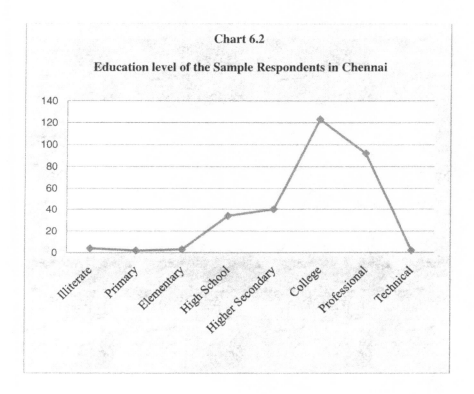

Table 6.7 shows the occupational status of the sample respondents in the study area. As per the data all the respondents are employed with the highest of private sector (32.3 percent) followed by Government (20.7 percent), business (20.3 percent), professinals (15 percent), sklled labour (6.7 percent) and self-employed (5 percent). Chart 6.3 presents the occupatinal status of the sample respondents in the study area.

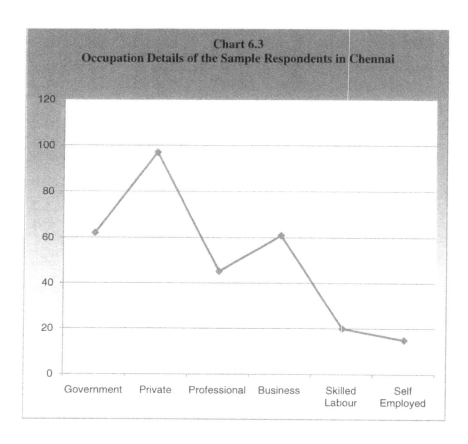

**Chart 6.3**
**Occupation Details of the Sample Respondents in Chennai**

## TYPE OF FAMILY

### Table 6.8
### Type of family of the Sample Respondents in Chennai

| Sl.No | Type of family | Frequency | Percent | Valid Percent | Cumulative Percent |
|-------|----------------|-----------|---------|---------------|--------------------|
| 1 | Joint | 58 | 19.3 | 19.3 | 19.3 |
| 2 | Nuclear | 242 | 80.7 | 80.7 | 100.0 |
| | Total | 300 | 100.0 | 100.0 | |

**Source: Computed from primary data**

Table 6.8 porrays that among the sample borrowers 19.3 percent are joint family and 80.7 percent are nuclear family. The majority of the sample borrowers are following nuclear type family which is due to migaration from other areas.

## HOUSE DETAILS

### Table 6.9
### Type of House of the Sample Respondents in Chennai

| Sl.No | Construction or Bought | Frequency | Percent | Valid Percent | Cumulative Percent |
|-------|------------------------|-----------|---------|---------------|--------------------|
| 1 | Purchased a constructed house | 67 | 22.3 | 22.3 | 22.3 |
| 2 | Purchased a built flat | 142 | 47.3 | 47.3 | 69.7 |
| 3 | Constructed house | 82 | 27.3 | 27.3 | 97.0 |
| 4 | Purchased through auction | 9 | 3.0 | 3.0 | 100.0 |
| | Total | 300 | 100.0 | 100.0 | |

**Source: Computed from primary data**

Table 6.9 shows that 47.3 percent of the sample borrowers have purchased built flat, 27.3 percent of them have built their house with the help of labourers and supervisors, 22.3 percent have purchased a constructed house and three percent have purchased their house through auction. The data indicates that the independent house either built directly or purchased second hand are more than flat owners and auctioned house. Chart 6.4 presents the details of the house of the sample respondents in the study area.

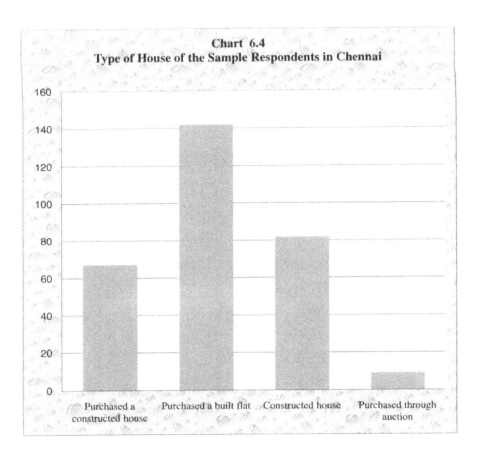

194

**Chart 6.4**
**Type of House of the Sample Respondents in Chennai**

## AGE OF THE HOUSE

Table 6.10
**Age of House of the Sample Respondents in Chennai (in years)**

| Sl.No | Age in years | Frequency | Percent | Valid Percent | Cumulative Percent |
|-------|--------------|-----------|---------|---------------|--------------------|
| 1 | 1 | 22 | 7.3 | 7.3 | 7.3 |
| 2 | 2 | 1 | 0.3 | 0.3 | 7.7 |
| 2 | 2 | 203 | 67.7 | 67.7 | 75.3 |
| 3 | 3 | 22 | 7.3 | 7.3 | 82.7 |
| 4 | 4 | 14 | 4.7 | 4.7 | 87.3 |
| 5 | 5 | 13 | 4.3 | 4.3 | 91.7 |
| 6 | 6 | 6 | 2.0 | 2.0 | 93.7 |
| 7 | 7 | 3 | 1.0 | 1.0 | 94.7 |
| 8 | 8 | 3 | 1.0 | 1.0 | 95.7 |
| 10 | 10 | 10 | 3.3 | 3.3 | 99.0 |
| 11 | 12 | 2 | 0.7 | 0.7 | 99.7 |
| 12 | 18 | 1 | 0.3 | 0.3 | 100.0 |
| | Total | 300 | 100.0 | 100.0 | |

**Source: Computed from primary data**

Table 6.10 portays that the majority of the house are two years old (67.7 percent) followed by one year and three years old (7.3 percent), four years (4.7 percent), five years (4.3 percent), then years (3.3 percent) and the rest are less than two years old.

PLINTH AREA

Table 6.11
Plinth area of dwelling unit of the Sample Respondents in
Chennai (in sq.ft)

| Sl.No | Plinth area | Frequency | Percent | Valid Percent | Cumulative Percent |
|-------|-------------|-----------|---------|---------------|--------------------|
| 1 | Below 400 | 2 | 0.7 | 0.7 | 0.7 |
| 2 | 400-700 | 128 | 42.7 | 42.7 | 43.3 |
| 2 | 700-1000 | 111 | 37.0 | 37.0 | 80.3 |
| 3 | 1000-1200 | 39 | 13.0 | 13.0 | 93.3 |
| 4 | 1200-2000 | 14 | 4.7 | 4.7 | 98.0 |
| 5 | Above 2000 | 6 | 2.0 | 2.0 | 100.0 |
| | Total | 300 | 100.0 | 100.0 | |

Source: Computed from primary data

The plinth area of the sample respondents presented in Table 6.11 shows that the majority of the dwelling units are in the range of 400 to 700 (42.7 percent) square foot followed by 700-1000 square foot (37 percent), 1000 to 1200 square foot (13 percent), 1200 to 2000 suare foot (4.7 percent) and the rest of two percent own in the range of above 2000 square foot.

SOURCES OF INCOME

Table 6.12
Sources of income of the Sample Respondents in Chennai

| Sl.No | Sources | Frequency | Percent | Valid Percent | Cumulative Percent |
|-------|---------|-----------|---------|---------------|--------------------|
| 1 | Salary | 190 | 63.3 | 63.3 | 63.3 |
| 2 | Business Income | 58 | 19.3 | 19.3 | 82.7 |
| 2 | Salary of Spouse | 15 | 5.0 | 5.0 | 87.7 |
| 3 | Self employment | 36 | 12.0 | 12.0 | 99.7 |
| 4 | Other Income | 1 | 0.3 | 0.3 | 100.0 |
| | Total | 300 | 100.0 | 100.0 | |

Source: Computed from primary data

Table 6.12 shows that of the sample respondents income from salary is the highest of 63.3 percent followed by 19.3 percent from business, 12 percent from self employment, five percent from spouse salary and 0.3 percent from other sources like shares, rent etc.

## LIC HOUSING FINANCE LIMITED AND LOANS

In this section of this thesis, the opinion of the sample respondents on the aspects of how they know about the existence of this institution, reason that have influenced you to prefer this institution, amount sanctioned as loan for purchase of the house/flat, rate of interest charged by the institution and type of interest rate preferred are discussed.

**Table 6.13**
**How the Sample Respondents Know about the Institution in the Study Area**

| Sl.No | Sources | Frequency | Percent | Valid Percent | Cumulative Percent |
|-------|---------|-----------|---------|---------------|--------------------|
| 1 | News Paper | 79 | 26.3 | 26.3 | 26.3 |
| 2 | Friends | 129 | 43.0 | 43.0 | 69.3 |
| 3 | Media Publicity | 90 | 30.0 | 30.0 | 99.3 |
| 4 | Others | 2 | 0.7 | 0.7 | 100.0 |
| | Total | 300 | 100.0 | 100.0 | |

**Source: Computed from primary data**

Table 6.13 portrays that 43 percent knew about LICHFL through their friends, 30 percent from media publicity, 26.3 percent from news paper and 0.7 percent from other sources like agents, officials etc.

**Table 6.14**
**Reason for Preference of the Institution by the**
**Sample Respondents in the Study Area**

| Sl.No | Reasons | Frequency | Percent | Valid Percent | Cumulative Percent |
|-------|---------|-----------|---------|---------------|---------------------|
| 1 | Low Rate of Interest | 102 | 34.0 | 34.0 | 34.0 |
| 2 | Easy Installments | 110 | 36.7 | 36.7 | 70.7 |
| 3 | Simple Formalities and Procedures | 81 | 27.0 | 27.0 | 97.7 |
| 4 | Other reasons | 7 | 2.3 | 2.3 | 100.0 |
| | Total | 300 | 100.0 | 100.0 | |

**Source: Computed from primary data**

Table 6.14 shows that 36.7 percent of the sample respondents have preferred LICHFL due to easy installments, 34 percent due to low rate of interest, 27 percent due to simple formalities and procedure, and the rest of 2.3 percent due to other reasons like life cover along with housing loan etc.

**Table 6.15**
**Purpose of Loan by the Sample Respondents in the Study Area**

| Sl.No | Purpose | Frequency | Percent | Valid Percent | Cumulative Percent |
|-------|---------|-----------|---------|---------------|---------------------|
| 1 | Purchase of House | 128 | 42.7 | 42.7 | 42.7 |
| 2 | Purchase of Flat | 110 | 36.7 | 36.7 | 79.3 |
| 3 | Construction of House | 59 | 19.7 | 19.7 | 99.0 |
| 4 | Other purpose | 3 | 1.0 | 1.0 | 100.0 |
| | Total | 300 | 100.0 | 100.0 | |

**Source: Computed from primary data**

Loan for purchase of the house or flat by the sample respondents in the study area is presented in Table 6.15. 42.7 percent of the borrowing for the purchase of house, 36.7 percent for the purpose of purchase flat, 19.7 percent for construction of house and one percent for other purpose like renovation etc.

**Table 6.16**
**Loan Amount Borrowed from LICHFL by the Sample Respondents in the Study Area (in rupees)**

| Sl. No | Loan | Frequency | Percent | Valid Percent | Cumulative Percent |
|--------|------|-----------|---------|---------------|--------------------|
| 1 | <300000 | 19 | 6.3 | 6.3 | 6.3 |
| 2 | 300001-600000 | 95 | 31.7 | 31.7 | 38.0 |
| 3 | 600001-900000 | 103 | 34.3 | 34.3 | 72.3 |
| 4 | 900001-1200000 | 21 | 7.0 | 7.0 | 79.3 |
| 5 | 1200001-1500000 | 28 | 9.3 | 9.3 | 88.6 |
| 6 | 1500001-1800000 | 4 | 1.3 | 1.3 | 89.9 |
| 7 | >1800001 | 30 | 10.1 | 10.1 | 100.0 |
| | Total | 300 | 100.0 | 100.0 | |

**Source: Computed from primary data**

Table 6.16 shows that 34.3 percent of the sample respondents have borrowed loan from LICHFL in the range of Rs. 600,001-900,000, 31.7 percent in the range of Rs. 300,001-600,000, 10.1 percent above Rs.18,00,001, 9.3 percent in the range of Rs. 12,00,001-15,00,000, 7 percent in the range of less than Rs.300,000, and 1.3 percent in the range of 15,00,001-18,00,000. Chart 6.5 presents the loan details of the sample respondents in the study area.

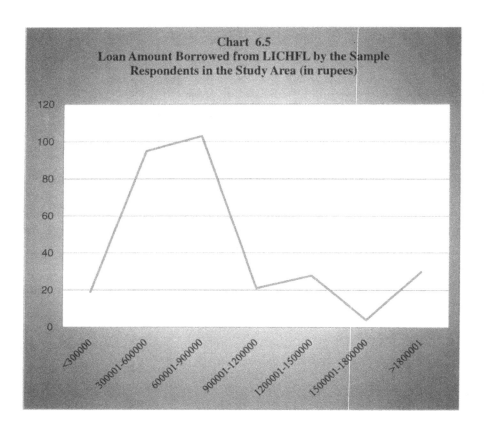

**Chart 6.5**
**Loan Amount Borrowed from LICHFL by the Sample**
**Respondents in the Study Area (in rupees)**

Table 6.17
Type of Interest Chosen by the Sample Respondents in the Study Area

| Sl.No | Type | Frequency | Percent | Valid Percent | Cumulative Percent |
|---|---|---|---|---|---|
| 1 | Fixed Rate | 35 | 11.7 | 11.7 | 11.7 |
| 2 | Floating Rate | 265 | 88.3 | 88.3 | 100.0 |
| | Total | 300 | 100.0 | 100.0 | |

Source: Computed from primary data

The borrowers of housing loan from LICHFL are given two options at the of taking loan viz., fixed rate and floating rate. As shown in Table 6.17 among the borrowers the majority of 88.3 percent have opted floating rate and the rest of 11.7 percent have chosen fixed rate.

## REPAYMENT OF LOAN

In this section of the thesis, the details of document properties reasonable period bulk repayment mode of payment second mortgage restricting the loan concessions and incentive benefits under the income tax residential status of your new house ideas for the development of housing sector suggested your friend or relative home loan account foreclosure of loan are discussed.

Table 6.18
Document Properties of the Sample Respondents in the Study Area

| Sl.No | Document property | Frequency | Percent | Valid Percent | Cumulative Percent |
|---|---|---|---|---|---|
| 1 | Mortgage of Finance | 54 | 18.0 | 18.0 | 18.0 |
| 2 | Life Insurance Policy Equal to the Loan Sanctioned | 80 | 26.7 | 26.7 | 44.7 |
| 3 | Deposit of the Title Deed | 134 | 44.7 | 44.7 | 89.3 |
| 4 | Additional Collateral as Security | 30 | 10.0 | 10.0 | 99.3 |
| 5 | Other | 2 | 0.7 | 0.7 | 100.0 |
| | Total | 300 | 100.0 | 100.0 | |

Source: Computed from primary data

Table 6.18 shows that 44.7 percent have preferred deposit of the title deed, 26.7 percent have taken LIC policy equal to the loan amount sanctioned, 18 percent have mortagage of finance, and 0.7 percent have additional collateral security.

**Table 6.19**
**Period of Loan Borrowed of the Sample Respondents in the Study Area**

| Sl.No | Loan period | Frequency | Percent | Valid Percent | Cumulative Percent |
|---|---|---|---|---|---|
| 1 | More Than 5 Years | 24 | 8.0 | 8.0 | 8.0 |
| 2 | More Than 10 Years | 156 | 52.0 | 52.0 | 60.0 |
| 3 | More Than 15 Years | 120 | 40.0 | 40.0 | 100.0 |
| | Total | 300 | 100.0 | 100.0 | |

**Source: Computed from primary data**

Table 6.19 portrays that the majority of 52 percent have borrowed loan for a period of more than 10 years, 40 percent for more than 15 years and eight percent for more than five years.

**Table 6.20**
**Bulk Payment Facility to the Borrowers of the LICHFL in the Study Area**

| Sl.No | Payment | Frequency | Percent | Valid Percent | Cumulative Percent |
|---|---|---|---|---|---|
| 1 | Yes | 90 | 30.0 | 30.0 | 30.0 |
| 2 | No | 210 | 70.0 | 70.0 | 100.0 |
| | Total | 300 | 100.0 | 100.0 | |

**Source: Computed from primary data**

Table 6.20 shows that 70 percent have said no and 30 percent said yes for the made bulk repayment facility during the loan period.

**Table 6.21**
**Mode of Payment by the Borrowers to the LICHFL in the Study Area**

| Sl. No | Mode of payment | Frequency | Percent | Valid Percent | Cumulative Percent |
|---|---|---|---|---|---|
| 1 | Salary Deduction | 70 | 23.3 | 23.3 | 23.3 |
| 2 | ECS | 144 | 48.0 | 48.0 | 71.3 |
| 3 | Post Dated Cheques | 68 | 22.7 | 22.7 | 94.0 |
| 4 | Collecting Bank | 18 | 6.0 | 6.0 | 100.0 |
| | Total | 300 | 100.0 | 100.0 | |

Source: Computed from primary data

Table 6.21 portrays that 48 percent have preferred ECS scheme, 22.7 percent have chosen post dated cheques, 23.3 percent in salary deduction and six percent through collecting bank.

**Table 6.22**
**Second Mortgage by the Borrowers to the LICHFL in the Study Area**

| Sl.No | Mortgage | Frequency | Percent | Valid Percent | Cumulative Percent |
|---|---|---|---|---|---|
| 1 | Yes | 75 | 25.0 | 25.0 | 25.0 |
| 2 | No | 225 | 75.0 | 75.0 | 100.0 |
| | Total | 300 | 100.0 | 100.0 | |

Source: Computed from primary data

Table 6.22 shows that 75 percent of the sample respondents said no and 25 percent said yes for their awareness about the second mortgage of loan. This exhibits that the majority of them are not aware of second mortgage of loan in the study area.

Table 6.23
Reason for Restricting the Loan Amount by the Borrowers to the
LICHFL in the Study Area

| Sl.No | Loan | Frequency | Percent | Valid Percent | Cumulative Percent |
|---|---|---|---|---|---|
| 1 | High Rate of Interest for Higher Loan | 71 | 23.7 | 23.7 | 23.7 |
| 2 | Statutory Limits | 51 | 17.0 | 17.0 | 40.7 |
| 3 | Low Income and Repayment Difficulties | 116 | 38.7 | 38.7 | 79.3 |
| 4 | Policy of the Institution | 62 | 20.6 | 20.6 | 100.0 |
| | Total | 300 | 100.0 | 100.0 | |

Source: Computed from primary data

The reasons for restricting the loan amount even though the requirement is high are given in Table 6.23. This shows that 38.7 percent have said that low income and repayment difficulties, 23.7 percent said high rate of interest for higher loan, 20.3 percent said policy of the institution and 17 percent said it is due to statutory limits.

Table 6.24
Aware of Concession and Incentives provided in the Latest
Budget by the Borrowers in the Study Area

| Sl.No | Awareness | Frequency | Percent | Valid Percent | Cumulative Percent |
|---|---|---|---|---|---|
| 1 | Yes | 262 | 87.3 | 87.3 | 87.3 |
| 2 | No | 38 | 12.7 | 12.7 | 100.0 |
| | Total | 300 | 100.0 | 100.0 | |

Source: Computed from primary data

Awareness of concession and incentives provided in the latest budget by the borrowers in the study area given in Table 6.24 shows that 12.7 percent said no and 87.3 percent said yes, which means the majority of them are aware of the benefits.

**Table 6.25**
**Aware of Income Tax Benefits by the Borrowers in the Study Area**

| Sl.No | Awareness | Frequency | Percent | Valid Percent | Cumulative Percent |
|-------|-----------|-----------|---------|---------------|--------------------|
| 1 | Yes | 230 | 76.7 | 76.7 | 76.7 |
| 2 | No | 70 | 23.3 | 23.3 | 100.0 |
| | Total | 300 | 100.0 | 100.0 | |

**Source: Computed from primary data**

Table 6.25 portrays that 76.7 percent said yes and 23.3 percent said no with regard to the awareness of the income tax benefits from the loan. This shows high awareness level among the sample borrowers in the study area.

**Table 6.26**

**Residential Status of the Borrowers in the Study Area**

| Sl.No | Status | Frequency | Percent | Valid Percent | Cumulative Percent |
|-------|--------|-----------|---------|---------------|--------------------|
| 1 | Self Occupied | 265 | 88.3 | 88.3 | 88.3 |
| 2 | Rental | 35 | 11.7 | 11.7 | 100.0 |
| | Total | 300 | 100.0 | 100.0 | |

**Source: Computed from primary data**

Table 6.26 shows that 88.3 percent of the sample respondents are living in self occupied house and the rest of 11.7 percent lives in rental houses.

Table 6.27

Expectation of the Borrowers form the Government in the Study Area

| Sl.No | Expectation | Frequency | Percent | Valid Percent | Cumulative Percent |
|-------|-------------|-----------|---------|---------------|--------------------|
| 1 | Enabling Flow of Resources to Housing Sector | 67 | 22.3 | 22.3 | 22.3 |
| 2 | Liberalise Legal and Regulatory Regime | 40 | 13.3 | 13.3 | 35.7 |
| 3 | Make Land Reforms Easy | 108 | 36.0 | 36.0 | 71.7 |
| 4 | Expand Rural and Urban Infrastructure | 60 | 20.0 | 20.0 | 91.7 |
| 5 | Supply Land for Housing | 25 | 8.3 | 8.3 | 100.0 |
| | Total | 300 | 100.0 | 100.0 | |

Source: Computed from primary data

The expectations of the borrowers given in Table 6.27 portrays that 36 percent says that land reforms should be made easy followed by 22.3 percent for enabling flow of resources to housing sector, 20 percent for expand rural and urban infrastructure, 13.3 percent for liberalizing legal and regulatory regime and 8.3 percent for supply of land for housing.

Table 6.28

Suggestion to the Borrowers in the Study Area

| S.No | Suggestion | Frequency | Percent | Valid Percent | Cumulative Percent |
|------|------------|-----------|---------|---------------|--------------------|
| 1 | Yes | 276 | 92.0 | 92.0 | 92.0 |
| 2 | No | 24 | 8.0 | 8.0 | 100.0 |
| | Total | 300 | 100.0 | 100.0 | |

Source: Computed from primary data

Table 6.28 shows that 92 percent have said yes and 8 percent said no for the question on whether you have suggested your friends or relatives to approach this insitution for loan. Since the majority have said yes and they have a good opinion with the institution.

Table 6.29

**Opening of Home Loan Account by the Borrowers in the Study Area**

| Sl.No | Home loan | Frequency | Percent | Valid Percent | Cumulative Percent |
|-------|-----------|-----------|---------|---------------|--------------------|
| 1 | Yes | 235 | 78.3 | 78.3 | 78.3 |
| 2 | No | 65 | 21.7 | 21.7 | 100.0 |
| | Total | 300 | 100.0 | 100.0 | |

Source: Computed from primary data

Table 6.29 percent portrays that 78.3 percent said they have openend home loan account and only 21.7 percent have said they have not openend such accout.

Table 6.30

**Foreclosure of Loan by the Borrowers in the Study Area**

| Sl.No | Foreclosure | Frequency | Percent | Valid Percent | Cumulative Percent |
|-------|-------------|-----------|---------|---------------|--------------------|
| 1 | No penalty | 104 | 34.7 | 34.7 | 34.7 |
| 2 | Pay charges | 87 | 29.0 | 29.0 | 63.7 |
| 3 | No benefit | 109 | 42.3 | 42.3 | 100.0 |
| | Total | 300 | 100.0 | 100.0 | |

Source: Computed from primary data

As given in Table 6.30 about 42.3 percent no benefits in the foreclosure of loan while 34.7 percent have said no penalty and 29 percent have said they have pay charges.

## OPINION OF THE BORROWERS

### Table 6.31

**Opinion on Government Encouraging the Housing Finance Sector in the Study Area**

| Sl.No | Opinion | Frequency | Percent | Valid Percent | Cumulative Percent |
|-------|---------|-----------|---------|---------------|--------------------|
| 1 | Agree | 217 | 72.3 | 72.3 | 72.3 |
| 2 | Strongly agree | 49 | 16.3 | 16.3 | 88.7 |
| 3 | Disagree | 22 | 7.3 | 7.3 | 96.0 |
| 4 | Strongly Disagree | 6 | 2.0 | 2.0 | 98.0 |
| 5 | No Opinion | 6 | 2.0 | 2.0 | 100.0 |
| | Total | 300 | 100.0 | 100.0 | |

**Source: Computed from primary data**

Table 6.31 shows that about 88.7 percent give favourable opinion (agreed by 72.3 percent and strongly agreed by 16.3 percent) that the Government is encouraging the housing finance sector.

Table 6.32

Opinion on Officials Helpful when Approached for Loan

| Sl.No | Opinion | Frequency | Percent | Valid Percent | Cumulative Percent |
|---|---|---|---|---|---|
| 1 | Agree | 111 | 37.0 | 37.0 | 37.0 |
| 2 | Strongly agree | 120 | 40.0 | 40.0 | 77.0 |
| 3 | Disagree | 43 | 14.3 | 14.3 | 91.3 |
| 4 | Strongly Disagree | 13 | 4.3 | 4.3 | 95.7 |
| 5 | No Opinion | 13 | 4.3 | 4.3 | 100.0 |
| | Total | 300 | 100.0 | 100.0 | |

Source: Computed from primary data

Table 6.32 portrays that the majority of 77 percent give favourable opinion (agreed by 37 percent and strongly agreed by 40 percent) that the officials are helpful when they have approached for loan, while the disagreement is only by 18.3 percent of the sample respondents in the study area.

Table 6.33

Opinion on Loan Amount Covers the Entire Cost of Flat or House

| Sl.No | Opinion | Frequency | Percent | Valid Percent | Cumulative Percent |
|---|---|---|---|---|---|
| 1 | Agree | 59 | 19.7 | 19.7 | 19.7 |
| 2 | Strongly agree | 72 | 24.0 | 24.0 | 43.7 |
| 3 | Disagree | 112 | 37.3 | 37.3 | 81.0 |
| 4 | Strongly Disagree | 42 | 14.0 | 14.0 | 95.0 |
| 5 | No Opinion | 15 | 5.0 | 5.0 | 100.0 |
| | Total | 300 | 100.0 | 100.0 | |

Source: Computed from primary data

As given in Table 6.33 about 37.3 percent said they disagree and 14 percent said they strongly agree that the loan amount covers the entire cost of the flat or house. The agreement is 43.7 percent (agreed by 19.7 percent and strongly agreed by 24 percent) for this opinion.

## Table 6.34

### Opinion on Rate of Interest Charged is Reasonable

| Sl.No | Opinion | Frequency | Percent | Valid Percent | Cumulative Percent |
|-------|---------|-----------|---------|---------------|--------------------|
| 1 | Agree | 74 | 24.7 | 24.7 | 24.7 |
| 2 | Strongly agree | 98 | 32.7 | 32.7 | 57.3 |
| 3 | Disagree | 64 | 21.3 | 21.3 | 78.7 |
| 4 | Strongly Disagree | 55 | 18.3 | 18.3 | 97.0 |
| 5 | No Opinion | 9 | 3.0 | 3.0 | 100.0 |
| | Total | 300 | 100.0 | 100.0 | |

Source: Computed from primary data

Table 6.34 shows that the majority of 57.3 percent give agreement (agreed by 24.7 percent and strongly agreed by 32.7 percent) that the rate of interest charged is reasonable, while the disagreement by 39.6 percent of the sample respondents in the study area.

Table 6.35

Opinion on Rate of Interest Charged by other Institutions is Reasonable

| Sl.No | Opinion | Frequency | Percent | Valid Percent | Cumulative Percent |
|-------|---------|-----------|---------|---------------|--------------------|
| 1 | Agree | 93 | 31.0 | 31.0 | 31.0 |
| 2 | Strongly agree | 80 | 26.7 | 26.7 | 57.7 |
| 3 | Disagree | 66 | 22.0 | 22.0 | 79.7 |
| 4 | Strongly Disagree | 30 | 10.0 | 10.0 | 89.7 |
| 5 | No Opinion | 31 | 10.3 | 10.3 | 100.0 |
| | Total | 300 | 100.0 | 100.0 | |

Source: Computed from primary data

As found in Table 6.35 about 26.7 percent said they strongly agree and 31 percent said they agree that the rate of interest charged by other institution is reasonable. The disagreement is 32 percent (disagreed by 22 percent and agreed by 10 percent) for this opinion.

Table 6.36

Opinion on Government National Housing Policy can be Liberalised

| Sl.No | Opinion | Frequency | Percent | Valid Percent | Cumulative Percent |
|-------|---------|-----------|---------|---------------|--------------------|
| 1 | Agree | 124 | 41.3 | 41.3 | 41.3 |
| 2 | Strongly agree | 86 | 28.7 | 28.7 | 70.0 |
| 3 | Disagree | 29 | 9.7 | 9.7 | 79.7 |
| 4 | Strongly Disagree | 30 | 10.0 | 10.0 | 89.7 |
| 5 | No Opinion | 31 | 10.3 | 10.3 | 100.0 |
| | Total | 300 | 100.0 | 100.0 | |

Source: Computed from primary data

Table 6.36 portrays that the majority of 70 percent give favourable opinion (agreed by 41.3 percent and strongly agreed by 28.7 percent) that the Government national housing policy can be liberalised, while the disagreement is only by 19.7 percent of the sample respondents in the study area.

### Table 6.37
### Opinion on Satisfied with Existing Arrangements of Finance

| Sl.No | Opinion | Frequency | Percent | Valid Percent | Cumulative Percent |
|-------|---------|-----------|---------|---------------|--------------------|
| 1 | Agree | 209 | 69.7 | 69.7 | 69.7 |
| 2 | Strongly agree | 53 | 17.7 | 17.7 | 87.3 |
| 3 | Disagree | 26 | 8.7 | 8.7 | 96.0 |
| 4 | Strongly Disagree | 8 | 2.7 | 2.7 | 98.7 |
| 5 | No Opinion | 4 | 1.3 | 1.3 | 100.0 |
| | Total | 300 | 100.0 | 100.0 | |

Source: Computed from primary data

Table 6.37 about 69.7 percent said they agree and 17.7 percent said they strongly agree that they are satisfied with existing arrangements of finance. The disagreement is 11.4 percent (disagreed by 8.7 percent and agreed by 2.7 percent) for this opinion.

## PROBLEMS FACED BY BORROWERS

### Table 6.38

### Opinion on Covered by any Life Insurance Benefits

| Sl.No | Opinion | Frequency | Percent | Valid Percent | Cumulative Percent |
|-------|---------|-----------|---------|---------------|--------------------|
| 1 | Agree | 116 | 38.7 | 38.7 | 38.7 |
| 2 | Strongly agree | 110 | 36.7 | 36.7 | 75.3 |
| 3 | Disagree | 51 | 17.0 | 17.0 | 92.3 |
| 4 | Strongly Disagree | 5 | 1.7 | 1.7 | 94.0 |
| 5 | No Opinion | 18 | 6.0 | 6.0 | 100.0 |
| | Total | 300 | 100.0 | 100.0 | |

Source: Computed from primary data

The opinion on whether repayment period given by the institution is adequate is presented in Table 6.40. This shows that 63 percent said they agree (agreed by 32 percent and strongly agreed by 31 percent) and the disagreement by 35 percent (disagreed by 25.3 percent and strongly disagreed by 9.7 percent) and no opinion by two percent.

Table 6.41

Opinion on Regular in making Prompt Payment of Loan

| Sl.No | Opinion | Frequency | Percent | Valid Percent | Cumulative Percent |
|-------|---------|-----------|---------|---------------|--------------------|
| 1 | Agree | 136 | 45.3 | 45.3 | 45.3 |
| 2 | Strongly agree | 94 | 31.3 | 31.3 | 76.7 |
| 3 | Disagree | 25 | 8.3 | 8.3 | 85.0 |
| 4 | Strongly Disagree | 29 | 9.7 | 9.7 | 94.7 |
| 5 | No Opinion | 16 | 5.3 | 5.3 | 100.0 |
| | Total | 300 | 100.0 | 100.0 | |

Source: Computed from primary data

As given in Table 6.41 about 45.3 percent said they agree and 31.3 percent said they strongly agree that they are regular in making prompt payment of loan. The disagreement is by 18 percent (disagreed by 8.3 percent and strongly disagreed by 9.7 percent) for this opinion.

Table 6.42
Opinion on Method of Calculating EMI is Good

| Sl.No | Opinion | Frequency | Percent | Valid Percent | Cumulative Percent |
|-------|---------|-----------|---------|---------------|--------------------|
| 1 | Agree | 115 | 38.3 | 38.3 | 38.3 |
| 2 | Strongly agree | 73 | 24.3 | 24.3 | 62.7 |
| 3 | Disagree | 48 | 16.0 | 16.0 | 78.7 |
| 4 | Strongly Disagree | 31 | 10.3 | 10.3 | 89.0 |
| 5 | No Opinion | 33 | 11.0 | 11.0 | 100.0 |
| | Total | 300 | 100.0 | 100.0 | |

Source: Computed from primary data

The method of calculating equated monthly installment (EMI) is good is agreed by 62.7 percent (with agreement by 38.3 percent and strong disagreement by 24.3 percent), while the disagreement is by 26.3 percent (disagreed by 16 percent and strongly disagreed by 10.3 percent) and no opinion by 11 percent.

Table 6.43
Opinion on Delay in Sanction and Disbursement

| Sl.No | Opinion | Frequency | Percent | Valid Percent | Cumulative Percent |
|-------|---------|-----------|---------|---------------|--------------------|
| 1 | Agree | 215 | 71.7 | 71.7 | 71.7 |
| 2 | Strongly agree | 46 | 15.3 | 15.3 | 87.0 |
| 3 | Disagree | 31 | 10.3 | 10.3 | 97.3 |
| 4 | Strongly Disagree | 5 | 1.7 | 1.7 | 99.0 |
| 5 | No Opinion | 3 | 1.0 | 1.0 | 100.0 |
| | Total | 300 | 100.0 | 100.0 | |

Source: Computed from primary data

The opinion on delay in sanction and disbursement is given in Table 6.43, which shows that 87 percent said they agree (agreed by 71.7 percent and strongly agreed by 15.3 percent) and the disagreement by 12 percent (disagreed by 10.3 percent and strongly disagreed by 1.7 percent) and no opinion by one percent.

**Table 6.44**

**Opinion on Inadequate Guidance by the Institution**

| Sl.No | Opinion | Frequency | Percent | Valid Percent | Cumulative Percent |
|-------|---------|-----------|---------|---------------|--------------------|
| 1 | Agree | 91 | 30.3 | 30.3 | 30.3 |
| 2 | Strongly agree | 113 | 37.7 | 37.7 | 68.0 |
| 3 | Disagree | 78 | 26.0 | 26.0 | 94.0 |
| 4 | Strongly Disagree | 10 | 3.3 | 3.3 | 97.3 |
| 5 | No Opinion | 8 | 2.7 | 2.7 | 100.0 |
| | Total | 300 | 100.0 | 100.0 | |

**Source: Computed from primary data**

Table 6.44 about 30.3 percent said they agree and 37.7 percent said they strongly agree about inadequate guidance given by the Institution. The disagreement is 29.3 percent (disagreed by 26 percent and strongly disagreed by 3.3 percent) for this opinion.

Table 6.45

**Opinion on Cumbersome Procedure followed by the Institution**

| Sl.No | Opinion | Frequency | Percent | Valid Percent | Cumulative Percent |
|---|---|---|---|---|---|
| 1 | Agree | 103 | 34.3 | 34.3 | 34.3 |
| 2 | Strongly agree | 101 | 33.7 | 33.7 | 68.0 |
| 3 | Disagree | 67 | 22.3 | 22.3 | 90.3 |
| 4 | Strongly Disagree | 13 | 4.3 | 4.3 | 94.7 |
| 5 | No Opinion | 16 | 5.3 | 5.3 | 100.0 |
| | Total | 300 | 100.0 | 100.0 | |

Source: Computed from primary data

The opinion on cumbersome procedure followed by the institution is agreed by 68 percent (with agreement by 34.3 percent and strong disagreement by 33.7 percent), while the disagreement is by 26.6 percent (disagreed by 22.3 percent and strongly disagreed by 4.3 percent) and no opinion by 5.3 percent.

Table 6.46

**Opinion on Lack of Interest shown by Officials**

| Sl.No | Opinion | Frequency | Percent | Valid Percent | Cumulative Percent |
|---|---|---|---|---|---|
| 1 | Agree | 94 | 31.3 | 31.3 | 31.3 |
| 2 | Strongly agree | 114 | 38.0 | 38.0 | 69.3 |
| 3 | Disagree | 66 | 22.0 | 22.0 | 91.3 |
| 4 | Strongly Agree | 15 | 5.0 | 5.0 | 96.3 |
| 5 | No Opinion | 11 | 3.7 | 3.7 | 100.0 |
| | Total | 300 | 100.0 | 100.0 | |

Source: Computed from primary data

Table 6.46 portrays that 69.3 percent of the sample respondents have agreed (agreed by 31.3 percent and strongly agreed by 38 percent) that lack of interest shown by officials in the institution, whereas it is disagreed by 22 percent, strongly disagreed by five percent and no opinion by 3.7 percent.

Table 6.47

Opinion on Difficult to Get Security/Surety for the Loan

| Sl.No | Opinion | Frequency | Percent | Valid Percent | Cumulative Percent |
|-------|---------|-----------|---------|---------------|--------------------|
| 1 | Agree | 117 | 39.0 | 39.0 | 39.0 |
| 2 | Strongly agree | 84 | 28.0 | 28.0 | 67.0 |
| 3 | Disagree | 68 | 22.7 | 22.7 | 89.7 |
| 4 | Strongly Disagree | 12 | 4.0 | 4.0 | 93.7 |
| 5 | No Opinion | 19 | 6.3 | 6.3 | 100.0 |
| | Total | 300 | 100.0 | 100.0 | |

Source: Computed from primary data

The opinion on difficulty to get security or surety for the housing loan by the institution is agreed by 67 percent (with agreement by 39 percent and strong disagreement by 28 percent), while the disagreement is by 26.7 percent (disagreed by 22.7 percent and strongly disagreed by 4 percent) and no opinion by 6.3 percent.

Table 6.48
Opinion on Heavy Interest Rates by the Sample
Respondents in the Study Area

| Sl.No | Opinion | Frequency | Percent | Valid Percent | Cumulative Percent |
|---|---|---|---|---|---|
| 1 | Agree | 180 | 60.0 | 60.0 | 60.0 |
| 2 | Strongly agree | 64 | 21.3 | 21.3 | 81.3 |
| 3 | Disagree | 45 | 15.0 | 15.0 | 96.3 |
| 4 | Strongly Disagree | 4 | 1.3 | 1.3 | 97.7 |
| 5 | No Opinion | 7 | 2.3 | 2.3 | 100.0 |
| | Total | 300 | 100.0 | 100.0 | |

Source: Computed from primary data

Table 6.48 portrays that 81.3 percent of the sample respondents have agreed (agreed by 60 percent and strongly agreed by 21.3 percent) that the institution charges heavy interest, whereas it is disagreed by 21.3 percent, strongly disagreed by 1.3 percent and no opinion by 2.3 percent.

Table 6.49

Opinion on Inconvenient to Pay EMI by the Sample
Respondents in the Study Area

| Sl.No | Opinion | Frequency | Percent | Valid Percent | Cumulative Percent |
|---|---|---|---|---|---|
| 1 | Agree | 102 | 34.0 | 34.0 | 34.0 |
| 2 | Strongly agree | 106 | 35.3 | 35.3 | 69.3 |
| 3 | Disagree | 65 | 21.7 | 21.7 | 91.0 |
| 4 | Strongly Agree | 14 | 4.7 | 4.7 | 95.7 |
| 5 | No Opinion | 13 | 4.3 | 4.3 | 100.0 |
| | Total | 300 | 100.0 | 100.0 | |

Source: Computed from primary data

As given in Table 6.49 about 34 percent said they agree and 35.3 percent said they strongly agree that they face inconvenience to pay equated monthly installments. The disagreement is by 26.4 percent (disagreed by 21.7 percent and strongly disagreed by 4.7 percent) for this opinion.

Table 6.50
Opinion on Irrelevant Scrutinisation by the Institution

| Sl.No | Opinion | Frequency | Percent | Valid Percent | Cumulative Percent |
|---|---|---|---|---|---|
| 1 | Agree | 109 | 36.3 | 36.3 | 36.3 |
| 2 | Strongly agree | 87 | 29.0 | 29.0 | 65.3 |
| 3 | Disagree | 70 | 23.3 | 23.3 | 88.7 |
| 4 | Strongly Disagree | 12 | 4.0 | 4.0 | 92.7 |
| 5 | No Opinion | 22 | 7.3 | 7.3 | 100.0 |
| | Total | 300 | 100.0 | 100.0 | |

Source: Computed from primary data

Table 6.50 shows that 65.3 percent of the sample respondents have agreed (agreed by 36.3 percent and strongly agreed by 29 percent) that the institution follows irrelevant scrutinisation, whereas it is disagreed by 23.3 percent, strongly disagreed by four percent and no opinion by 7.3 percent.

Table 6.51
Opinion on Illogical Approach of the Institution

| Sl.No | Opinion | Frequency | Percent | Valid Percent | Cumulative Percent |
|---|---|---|---|---|---|
| 1 | Agree | 78 | 26.0 | 26.0 | 26.0 |
| 2 | Strongly agree | 82 | 27.3 | 27.3 | 53.3 |
| 3 | Disagree | 97 | 32.3 | 32.3 | 85.7 |
| 4 | Strongly Disagree | 21 | 7.0 | 7.0 | 92.7 |
| 5 | No Opinion | 22 | 7.3 | 7.3 | 100.0 |
| | Total | 300 | 100.0 | 100.0 | |

Source: Computed from primary data

The opinion on illogical approach followed by the institution for the housing loan is agreed by 53.3 percent (with agreement by 26 percent and strong disagreement by 27.3 percent), while the disagreement is by 39.3 percent (disagreed by 32.3 percent and strongly disagreed by 7 percent) and no opinion by 7.3 percent.

Table 6.52

**Opinion on Difficult to Accomplish the Need within the Sanction Amount**

| Sl.No | Opinion | Frequency | Percent | Valid Percent | Cumulative Percent |
|-------|---------|-----------|---------|---------------|--------------------|
| 1 | Agree | 136 | 45.3 | 45.3 | 45.3 |
| 2 | Strongly agree | 75 | 25.0 | 25.0 | 70.3 |
| 3 | Disagree | 51 | 17.0 | 17.0 | 87.3 |
| 4 | Strongly Disagree | 19 | 6.3 | 6.3 | 93.7 |
| 5 | No Opinion | 19 | 6.3 | 6.3 | 100.0 |
| | Total | 300 | 100.0 | 100.0 | |

**Source: Computed from primary data**

Table 6.52 gives the opinion of the sample respondents to accomplish the need within the sanction amount. This shows that 70.3 percent (with agreement by 45.3 percent and strong disagreement by 25 percent), while the disagreement is by 23.3 percent (disagreed by 17 percent and strongly disagreed by 6.3 percent) and no opinion by 6.3 percent.

## TEST OF HYPOTHESES

**There is a significant increase in the disbursal of housing loan by the LIC Housing Finance Limited**

To test this hypothesis data pertaining to disbursal of housing loan (Table 5.3) by the LIC Housing Finance Limited is considered. To test the validity of the hypothesis t-test is followed as per the procedure given below.

$$t = \frac{(\bar{x} - \mu)\sqrt{n}}{S}$$

where $\bar{x}$ = the mean of the sample

$\mu$ = the actual or hypothetical mean of the population

$n$ = the sample size

$s$ = the standard deviation of the sample

$$s = \sqrt{\frac{\Sigma (X - X)^2}{n - 1}}$$

Ho = There is no significant increase in the disbursal of housing loan by the LIC Housing Finance Limited.

$H_1$ = There is significant increase in the disbursal of housing loan by the LIC Housing Finance Limited.

| t | df | Sig. (2-tailed) | Mean Difference | 95% Confidence Interval of the Difference | |
|---|---|---|---|---|---|
| | | | | Lower | Upper |
| 4.936 | 9 | .001 | 2306.4180 | 11249.4115 | 3363.4245 |

The computed value t = 4.936 and the table value ($t_{0.05}$ = 1.833) is more than the computed value and hence the hypothesis is rejected. As a result it is inferred that there is significant increase in the disbursal of housing loan by the LIC Housing Finance Limited.

**There is a significant improvement in the financial position of LIC Housing Finance Limited.**

To test this hypothesis data pertaining to financial position (Table 5.1) by the LIC Housing Finance Limited is considered. To test the validity of the hypothesis t-test is followed as per the procedure for the first hypothesis is used.

Ho = There is no significant increase in the total income of the LIC Housing Finance Limited.

$H_1$ = There is significant increase in the total income of the LIC Housing Finance Limited.

| t | df | Sig. (2-tailed) | Mean Difference | 95% Confidence Interval of the Difference | |
|---|---|---|---|---|---|
| | | | | Lower | Upper |
| 9.115 | 9 | .000 | 802.5620 | 603.3767 | 1001.7473 |

The computed value t = 9.115 and the table value ($t_{0.05}$ = 1.833) is more than the computed value and hence the hypothesis is rejected. As a result it is inferred that there is significant increase in the total income of the LIC Housing Finance Limited.

**The beneficiaries are happy with the services provided by LIC Housing Finance Limited**

To test this hypothesis data pertaining to borrowers of loan from the LIC Housing Finance Limited is considered. To test the validity of the hypothesis t-test is followed as per the procedure given below.

Ho = There is no significant difference in the happiness with the services provided by the LIC Housing Finance Limited.

$H_1$ = There is significant difference in the happiness with the services provided by the LIC Housing Finance Limited.

| t | df | Sig. (2-tailed) | Mean Difference | 95% Confidence Interval of the Difference | |
|---|---|---|---|---|---|
| | | | | Lower | Upper |
| 1.569 | 4 | 0.192 | 60.0000 | -46.1713 | 166.1713 |

The computed value t = 1.569 and the table value ($t_{0.05}$ = 2.132) is less than the computed value and hence the null hypothesis is accepted. As a result it is inferred that there is no significant difference in the happiness with the services provided by the LIC Housing Finance Limited.

**The beneficiaries are aware of the rules of the LIC Housing Finance Limited.**

To test this hypothesis data pertaining to borrower's awareness of rules of LIC Housing Finance Limited is considered. To test the validity of the hypothesis chi-square test is followed.

1. Hypotheses:

   Ho = There is no significant difference in the awareness of the rules of the LIC Housing Finance Limited.

   $H_1$ = There is significant difference in the awareness of the rules of the LIC Housing Finance Limited.

2. Critical region: Reject H0 It $\chi^2 \geq \chi^2$ value with (n-1) df at 5% level of significance.

3. Computed value   :

| | Aware of concession and incentives |
|---|---|
| Chi-Square | 167.253 |
| df | 1 |
| Asymp. Sig. | .000 |

The computed value of $\chi = 167.253$ is more than the table value ($\chi_{05}=3.84$) and hence the null hypothesis is rejected. As a result it is inferred that there is significant difference in the awareness among the borrowers in the rules of the LIC Housing Finance Limited.

**There is a significant difference in the opinion of the beneficiaries on their loan requirement and loan sanctioned by the LIC Housing Finance Limited.**

To test this hypothesis data pertaining to borrower's loan requirement and the total amount of loan sanctioned by the LIC Housing Finance Limited is considered. To test the validity of the hypothesis ANOVA one way method is followed.

Ho = There is no significant difference between loan requirement and loan sanctioned by the LIC Housing Finance Limited.

$H_1$ = There is significant difference between loan requirement and loan sanctioned by the LIC Housing Finance Limited.

|  | Sum of Squares | df | Mean Square | F | Sig. |
|---|---|---|---|---|---|
| Between Groups | 6.359 | 4 | 1.590 | 1.313 | .265 |
| Within Groups | 357.228 | 295 | 1.211 |  |  |
| Total | 363.587 | 299 |  |  |  |

The computed value of $F = 1.313$ is more than the table value (5.6281) and hence the null hypothesis is rejected. As a result it is inferred that there is significant difference between loan requirement and loan sanctioned by the LIC Housing Finance Limited.

# SUMMARY & CONCLUSION

# CHAPTER VII

## SUMMARY AND CONCLUSION

Housing is a global problem. As a corollary of poverty, this is a chronic problem in the developing countries. The very low levels of income of the vast majority of the population and the spurt in population have been increasing the dimensions of the housing problem in India. The housing problem is not a mere demand-supply problem. Because of the poor income of majority of the households, there is bound to be a wide gap between the demand for houses and the need for houses because the need is translated into demand only when it is backed by purchasing power. Majority of households, being so poor that they cannot afford even the cheapest dwellings available, a mere increase in the supply of houses will not solve the problem, though it can alleviate the problem. The resource constraints and magnitude of the problem indicate the limitations of free or subsidized housing scheme in making a major dent on the problem.

The magnitude and dimensions of the problem clearly indicate that the housing problem in India cannot be completely solved in the short run. Effective solution to problem calls for a long-term strategy with the needed sub strategies and short term strategies incorporated to it. The Government has been paying particular attention to mitigate the housing problem of the economically weaker sections. A considerable part of the money spent on the public housing projects is said to be pilfered by the unscrupulous. Overestimating the cost and use of substandard and spurious materials appear to be widespread. A housing policy to be effective should consider the income levels and capacity to pay of the households.

Housing is a complex, multi dimensional commodity. As a durable asset, housing structure provides both consumption and investment services and can be purchased with loan or other form of assistance. Finance is thus provided for the house construction, purchase of house or flat or plot, for repairs and renewals or extension of already existing houses. Many housing finance companies are in existence with different schemes and with different purposes of loan, which an individual can access to own a house.

The importance of housing finance as an important component of housing delivery system was recognized in the 1970. It was, however, only around the launching of the Seventh Five Year Plan that the need for developing a responsive housing finance system was felt. It was felt that for the development of a housing finance system, a national level apex housing finance institution, having functions of co-ordinaton and regulation of the sector, would be an essential pre-requisite.

LIC Housing Finance Limited is one of India's second largest housing finance institution. This institution from its inception has taken customer service as its foremost aim. This institution provides sufficient housing loans to its customers, so that their dreams of owning a house are fulfilled. This institution not only provides housing loans to individuals but also to state government, Tamilnadu Housing Board, Co-operative Societies, Corporate Builders and Other Developers too

India is a country of large and the fastest growing population in the world, with more than one thousand million population and growing number of metropolitan cities. The Chennai city being one of the major urban metropolis in the country has an acute shortage of not only infrastructure but more so of housing. The public and private sector with an impetus given in the several Five Year Plans have done their level best to meet the shortages and to remove the deficit of housing.

The Housing Financial Institutions have played a major role since nearly past two decades and have been responsible to access finance over the years. Institutions providing housing finance in the city of Chennai have discriminated the consumer in respect of sanctioning of loans, thereby concentrating on certain benchmark with respect to income level. This discrimination is primarily due to the risk factors involved and insufficient foreclosure norms that exist today.

In these circumstances, an attempt is made in this thesis to study the role of LIC Housing Finance Limited in providing housing finance. The major objectives of the study in chapter one were to trace the housing finance system and policies in India, to analyse the changing role of housing financial institutions to review the performance of the operational and financial position of LIC housing Finance Limited to elicit the opinion of the urban beneficiaries of LIC Housing Finance Limited and to suggest the measures to improve the efficiency of LIC Housing Finance Limited.

The present study covered the period between the years from 1996 to 2006. The database for the research consisted of primary and secondary data. The primary data were collected through pre-tested questionnaires from the beneficiaries of LIC Housing finance Limited. The five year plans of Government of India and the growth of housing finance sector from a part of the chapter in introducing, defining and explaining the problem under study. A set of hypothesis is framed to study the factors involved.

The necessary secondary data were collected from various sources like census reports, city profile, statistical tables relating to housing, five-year plan documents of Government of India, Annual reports and conference proceedings of LIC Housing Finance Limited, other relevant reports and articles from various journals. Hypotheses were framed and relevant statistical tools to test the hypotheses were used. The study has been presented in seven chapters. They are Introduction, Review of Literature, Profile of the Study Area, Housing Finance-An Overview, Performance analysis of LIC Housing Finance Limited, Analysis of beneficiaries responses and Summary of Findings and Conclusion.

In the second chapter, a brief review of ninety studies on aspects covering the Homelessness and Housing Problem, Trends in urbanization, Government participation in housing, Housing policy, Housing Finance and Investment and Institutions providing housing finance. Housing problem and the trends in urbanization analysed in the chapter are the contributions of Cooper, Daly, Epstein, Charles Abrams, Betrand Renand, Hawley, Nelson, Victor, and Smita Sengupta. In the studies on Government participation in housing, Housing policy, Housing Finance and Investment and Institutions providing housing finance several studies of World Bank and by Indians are given. In the studies under Housing Finance and Investment, Renault Betrand has made a study of the housing and financial institutions in developing countries. He has identified that the weak existence of borrowed capital in the developing countries is the main cause for the inadequate development of housing financial development. He has concluded saying that the problem of housing finance could be solved only through reconciling three conflicting objectives: improve competitions, increase efficiency and stimulate long term finance. Studies reviewed in this chapter reveal certain gaps that provide ample scope for a researcher to pursue this topic for further research.

Chapter Three has dealt with the profile of the study area. Chennai city was chosen as the area of study. This was done purposively because the city of Chennai is one of the major urban metropolis in the country having acute shortage of not only infrastructure but also housing. The discussion about the study area was grouped under the following heads namely Evolution of Chennai City, Geographical and physical background, General profile of Chennai City, Demographic background, Infrastructural facilities and amenities and Housing development in Chennai City. The city of Chennai, which was the fourth largest city in the country in terms of population during 1991, moved to fifth place during 2001. Chennai City being the capital of Tamil Nadu accounts for around 6.78 percent of State population amounting to 42,16,268. The distribution of male and female in the total population is 21,61,605 (6.9 percent of State male population) and 20,54,663 (6.7 percent of State female population). Chennai has 951 females for every male. The sex ratio per 1000 males in Chennai has increased from 934 during 1991 to 951 during 2001. The Population density that was 5832 persons per square kilometer during 1871 Increased to 24231 persons in the year 2001. Out 4.16 lakhs population, about 30.79 lakhs are literates (Table 3.12) resulting in a reduction of literacy rate from 81.60 per cent during 1991 to 80.14 per cent during 2001. The male literacy rate has come down from 87.86 percent to 84.71 percent but there is slight increase in female literacy rate going to 75.32 percent in 2001 from 74.87 percent during 1991. Nevertheless the total literates in Chennai have increased from 27.52 lakhs to 47.69 lakhs resulting in an increase of about 73 percent. Among the districts of Tamilnadu, Chennai with 80.14 percent ranks 4th in literacy, 1st, 2nd and 3rd being Kanyakumari, Thuthukudi, and Nilgiris with 88.11 percent, 81.96 percent, and 81.44 percent respectively. However Chennai district has registered higher literacy rate than the state average of 73.4 %. As per the latest census reports, Chennai has 14.41 lakhs workers of which about 80 per cent are males and the rest are females. Obviously, all these workers belong either to secondary or tertiary categories, and the proportion of primary workers is very much insignificant.

Chennai City is well connected to other places of the state and to major towns and state headquarters of neighboring states by road, rail and also by air. Thus, the population that moves in or out of the city runs into a few lakhs. Chennai is recognized as one of the National Commission of Urbanization (NCU). Because of its primacy, Chennai tends to grow faster and bigger, in the context of liberalized economy. Focus on Industrial Development and entry of Multi National Companies in Industrial Sector, the pace of development of Chennai Metropolitan Area is likely to be faster. This warrants urgent measures to plan, implement and guide the developments in order to make the Metropolitan Area livable by improving its quality of life. Chennai Metropolitan Development Authority focuses its activities on various development schemes with the above concept in mind. In 1961 the Government created the Tamil Nadu Housing Board (TNHB), reflecting the fact that the rural-urban migration and natural increase in population in Chennai were escalating the demand for housing well above the supply.

In fourth chapter an overview of housing finance is presented in terms of Trends of Urbanization in India, Housing in India, Housing Scenario during the plan period, Housing Finance – A Global perspective, Housing Finance System and policy in India, Institutions providing housing finance. In the decade 1991-2001, the growth of urban population is 31.40, and it again declined by 5 points than the earlier decade. The growth rate has been declined since 1981. The reason for this slowing down of growth rate is due to slowness in economic development. Gaining an idea about the present situation relating housing is a precondition to plan for the future development of housing. Most of the people in India are homeless. They live only in rental houses without adequate amenities like water, toilets, etc. Increase in population has contributed to the heavy demand for houses in India, which in turn has resulted in the increased demand for financial assistance from the organised finance institutions.

Table 4.2 reveals that the shortage of houses has increased from 8.9 million in 1951 to 45.9 million in 2001. Even the analysis with regard to housing shortage of urban and rural areas also reflects that the shortage of houses has increased to more than 400 per cent. Increase in the shortage of housing between urban and rural areas is comparatively higher than that in the urban areas. From the analysis it is clear that because of the increase in the population in our country, the shortage of houses has also gone up. For meeting the acute challenge situation in the country, there is a vital need for evolving an efficient planning technique for designing and execution of schemes with utmost achievement of economy and speedy action-oriented programme of quick decisive policies.

India's population has already crossed a mark of 1 billion and it is estimated that by the year 2021, 350 million people will be added with further concentration of population in urban center up to 12 percent. According to Census of 2001, India had total residential housing stock of 187 million with only 51 percent permanent dwelling units. Furthermore, out of this housing stock 54 per cent have no sanitation facility, nearly 85% do not have electricity and more than 22 per cent do not have drainage facility. The lack of basic infrastructure facilities in present housing stock and the shortfall indicates chronic shortage of dwelling units with basic needs. Moreover, it is estimated that by the year 2021 the population of urban poor will be nearly 180 million.

Table 4.5 observed that that in successive Five-Year Plans the percentage of investment in housing has fallen from 34 per cent in the first Plan to 6 per cent in the Ninth Plan. Simultaneously around 1952, housing in private sector also started in and around Mumbai and Delhi. This was later on came to be known as Real Estate Industry. As the private sector started playing a dominant role, the Government role has been reduced to that of providing housing to Economically Weaker Sections (EWS). Low Income Group (LIG), and other needy and specified classes. Housing has been largely a people' activity. Its contribution to housing ranged from 73 percent in Third Five-Year Plan to as high as 91 per cent in the Seventh Five year Plan. As per the report of the working group on finance for housing sector for the

Eighth Plan, 80 per cent come from private savings and non-formal sources of credit. The large proportion of houses provided by householders themselves constitutes the informal private sector.

In India, the existing housing finance system is dominated by a series of special and general financial institutions. Amongst them, HUDCO(Housing and Urban Development Corporation) and HDFC(Housing Development Finance Corporation) are the specialized agencies, LIC(Life Insurance Corporation), GIC(General Insurance Corporation) and the commercial banks are the general ones. In terms of financial turnover, institutional sources account for only 10 per cent of total finance in the housing sector. Apart from this the informal sources of finance have a significant contribution to make. The formal sector institutions largely mobilize resources from general financial institutions leading to complex inter institutional flows.

Performance analysis of LIC Housing Finance Limited is discussed in Chapter five of the thesis. This chapter is divided into two heads viz., Financial performance of LIC Housing Finance Ltd and Operational performance of LIC Housing Finance Ltd.

Since the government finally recognized the utmost importance of housing finance in a developing economy like India where a large part of one billion strong population is still deprived of decent housing, the housing finance industry has assumed all the more significance, and by now 400 entities, including housing finance companies and banks – nationalized foreign and as well as co-operative have entered the scene. One such prominent company in this field is LIC Housing Finance Ltd, a subsidiary of LIC of India.

The institution follows the policy laid down by the NHB. The main objectives are to achieve the aim of "Shelter for homeless", to promote a sound, healthy, viable and the cost effective housing finance system, to cater to all segments of the population, to establish a network of housing finance outlets to adequately serve different regions and different income groups and to encourage the flow of credit and real sources to the small man first.

Table 5.1 clearly brings out the trends in the financial performance of the LIC Housing Finance Limited during the research period 1996-97 to 2005-06. In the year 1996-97 the company earned a total income of Rs.411.70 crores and registered a growth of 22 per cent, which has been increased to 1,268.83 crores in the year 2005-06 registering an increase of 20.78 per cent. The company recommended the dividend payment of 20 per cent in the year 1996-97, which rose to 60 per cent in the year 2005-06. The dividend payment has been tripled during the research period.

The company exhibits a fluctuating trend in the profitability measures during the study period 1996-97 to 2005-06. The liquidity position of the company has been showing satisfactory results, which is showing the ideal ratio. The earning per share of the company during the study period is in favourable position from 2000-01 to till the end of the study period, which is much higher than the normal rate of earning per share, which is 15 per cent. But the results of the other criteria are not satisfactory. It is to be mentioned here that the company has not incurred losses during any of the years covered under the study.

In the year 1996-97, the Company sanctioned loans for 788.41 crores and disbursed loans for Rs.739.67 crores, which has been increased to Rs.5027.28 crores and Rs.4.670.08 crores in the year 2005-2006. On the basis of compound growth rates, under region-wise disbursements it is analysed that the Eastern region ranks first in the disbursement of individual loans. It means the company's schemes of housing loans are flourishing well in this region. So far as portfolio amount and default figure are concerned, the Northern region occupies the first rank. This region has the lowest compound growth rate of defaults as compared to other regions. It means that the credit analysis, appraisal and management of this region are better. While analyzing the overall position of the company, it emerges that there is a need to bring down the default figures for its survival. Serious actions have not been taken up by some of the area officers such as western region, South Central region and Southern region at this front, and hence, it results into huge increase in defaults.

In Chapter six, an evaluation of the opinion of the housing loan borrowers of the LIC housing finance limited on identification, socio-economic and cultural status, LIC Housing Finance Limited and loans, repayment of loan, opinion of the borrowers, and problems faced by borrowers is presented. In this study, 86.7 percent of the sample borrowers are male and 13.3 percent of them are female. Among the borrowers 43.7 percent are Backward Class, 33 percent are Most Backward Class, 15 percent are Other Castes, 7.3 percent are Scheduled Castes and the rest of one percent are Scheduled Tribes. Of these 85.3 percent are Hindus, 10.3 percent are Christians, 2.7 percent are Muslims and 1.6 percent are others.

The educated sample respondents are more than illiterate. Of the educated, sample respondents studied college level is more than professionals, higher secondary and high school. All the respondents are employed with the highest of private sector (32.3 percent) followed by Government (20.7 percent), business (20.3 percent), profesinals (15 percent), sklled labour (6.7 percent) and self-employed (5 percent).

Among the sample borrowers 19.3 percent are joint family and 80.7 percent are nuclear family. 47.3 percent of the sample borrowers have purchased built flat, 27.3 percent of them have built their house with the help of labourers and supervisors, 22.3 percent have purchased a constructed house and three percent have purchased their house through auction. Of which, the majority of the house are two years old. The majority of the dwelling units are in the range of 400 to 700 (42.7 percent) square foot followed by 700-1000 square foot (37 percent), 1000 to 1200 square foot (13 percent), 1200 to 2000 suare foot (4.7 percent) and the rest of two percent own in the range of above 2000 square foot.

For the sample respondenst the income from salary is the highest of 63.3 percent followed by 19.3 percent from business, 12 percent from self employment, five percent from spouse salary and 0.3 percent from other sources like shares, rent etc. 36.7 percent of the sample respondents have preferred LICHFL due to easy installments, 34 percent due to low rate of interest and 27 percent due to simple formalities and procedure.

Of the borrowers, 42.7 percent of the borrowing for the purchase of house, 36.7 percent for the purpose of purchase flat, 19.7 percent for construction of house and one percent for other purpose like renovation etc. The majority of 88.3 percent have opted floating rate and the rest of 11.7 percent have chosen fixed rate. 44.7 percent have preferred deposit of the title deed, 26.7 percent have taken LIC policy equal to the loan amount sanctioned, 18 percent have mortagage of finance, and 0.7 percent have additional collateral security. The majority of 52 percent have borrowed loan for a period of more than 10 years, 40 percent for more than 15 years and eight percent for more than five years. In the repayment, about 48 percent have preferred ECS scheme, 22.7 percent have chosen post dated cheques, 23.3 percent in salary deduction and six percent through collecting bank.

The majority of them are aware of the benefits, the majority have said yes and they have a good opinion with the institution. The majority of 77 percent give favourable opinion that the officials are helpful when they have approached for loan. 57.3 percent of them give agreement that the rate of interest charged is reasonable. 69.7 percent said they agree and 17.7 percent said they strongly agree that they are satisfied with existing arrangements of finance. Among the borrowers, 45.3 percent said they agree and 31.3 percent said they strongly agree that they are regular in making prompt payment of loan.

Cumbersome procedure followed by the institution is agreed by 68 percent, while the disagreement is by 26.6 percent. Difficulty to get security or surety for the housing loan by the institution is agreed by 67 percent. 65.3 percent of the sample respondents have agreed that the institution follows irrelevant scrutinisation.

have opted floating rate and the rest of 11.7 percent have chosen fixed rate. 44.7 percent have preferred deposit of the title deed, 26.7 percent have taken LIC policy equal to the loan amount sanctioned, 18 percent have mortagage of finance, and 0.7 percent have additional collateral security. The majority of 52 percent have borrowed loan for a period of more than 10 years, 40 percent for more than 15 years and eight percent for more than five years. In the repayment, about 48 percent have preferred ECS scheme, 22.7 percent have chosen post dated cheques, 23.3 percent in salary deduction and six percent through collecting bank.

The majority of them are aware of the benefits. the majority have said yes and they have a good opinion with the institution. The majority of 77 percent give favourable opinion that the officials are helpful when they have approached for loan. 57.3 percent of them give agreement that the rate of interest charged is reasonable. 69.7 percent said they agree and 17.7 percent said they strongly agree that they are satisfied with existing arrangements of finance. Among the borrowers, 45.3 percent said they agree and 31.3 percent said they strongly agree that they are regular in making prompt payment of loan.

Cumbersome procedure followed by the institution is agreed by 68 percent, while the disagreement is by 26.6 percent. Difficulty to get security or surety for the housing loan by the institution is agreed by 67 percent. 65.3 percent of the sample respondents have agreed that the institution follows irrelevant scrutinisation.

**SUGGESTIONS**

Following are the suggestions to improve the performance of LIC Housing Finance Limited in providing Housing Finance and making it easily accessible to almost all beneficiaries of various income levels.

1. LIC Housing Finance Limited should reduce the rate of interest which is the most important factor in deciding the level of finance required especially in cities like Chennai.

2. EMI calculated on monthly reducing balance method will minimize the cost of loan and safeguard the borrower's hard earned money.

3. The company should not fix any age limit for the access to housing loan taking into consideration the mortgage of property or the collateral security provided by the borrower.

4. LIC Housing finance Company should accept payment of minimum margin amount and it should be allowed to be paid through credit cards as followed in other countries.

5. Steps should be initiated by the company like the secondary mortgage market or housing refinance schemes which will enhance accessibility and reduce the risk involved.

6. Housing loan organization should not charged for processing, administration, conversion fees and other charges for prepayment penalty.

7. Interest charges should be on daily reducing basis and should provide a flexibility to convert from fixed to floating or floating to fixed interest schedules.

8. Priority for financing housing should be provided to low-income families. But this finance should be appropriate and target the preferences of beneficiaries.

9. The procedures of credit of various types, eligibility to avail them, interest charged on them, mode of security, loan documents to be submitted and mode of repayment of loans of LIC Housing Finance Limited should be made known to the general public.

10. Cumbersome procedures in sanctioning the loan by the institution should be reduced.

CPSIA information can be obtained
at www.ICGtesting.com
Printed in the USA
LVHW112037270323
742731LV00020BA/519